"Dr. Griffin's work as a Church Consultant has been invaluable to our church. Our leadership has been revitalized. Our vision has been sharpened. His personalized usage of the Enneagram has helped us better understand and appreciate the unique qualities that we have in our church. This book is a must read for any and all pastors that desire to take their ministry to the next level."

Dr. Anthony Bennett
Mount Aery Baptist Church
Bridgeport, CT

"The G.P.S. (God's Positioning System) is an innovative transition resource that every new pastor should understand and implement!"

Dr. George Wilson, Sr. Pastor
Friends 4 Life Covenant Church
Flossmoor, IL

"Our church will never appoint another leader without using Dr. Griffin's Building a Better Team System!"

Pastor Bryndan Crawford Loritts
First Baptist Church of Lansing
Lansing, IL

"Dr. Griffin's statement, 'before there is any vision preaching there must be transition preaching,' was worth the conference."

Dr. Jocelyn Thornton, Sr. Pastor
Emmanuel Covenant Church
Orland Park, IL

NAVIGATING
PASTORAL
LEADERSHIP

IN THE
TRANSITION ZONE

"Arriving in the middle of the movie"

D. DARRELL GRIFFIN

NAVIGATING PASTORAL LEADERSHIP

IN THE
TRANSITION ZONE

"Arriving in the middle of the movie"

EDITED BY
DARRYL D. SIMS

MMGI BOOKS, CHICAGO, ILLINOIS

NAVIGATING PASTORAL LEADERSHIP IN THE TRANSITION ZONE

"Arriving in the middle of the movie"

Library of Congress Cataloging-in-Publication Data
Navigating Pastoral Leadership in the Transition Zone / church leadership and growth
By D. Darrell Griffin
    p. cm.
ISBN 978-0-615-266616-9 (pbk. :alk. Paper)
Church leadership 2) Religious life 3) Transitional methodology.

Printed in the U.S.A.

DEDICATION

This book would have never been written without the strength and grace of God, as well as the love, support, encouragement, and prayers of many faithful friends and family members.

To my wife, Chereese, and my sons, Miles and Bryce, who sacrificed so much for the sake of the Kingdom of God.

To my father, the late Charles Edward Griffin and to my mother, Juliette Bryant Griffin, and to my brothers, Dr. Anthony C., Michael, Kerry and Kelly.

To my in-laws who have become my family, Dr. and Mrs. Gene R. Newton and family.

To my Oakdale Covenant Church and Oakdale Christian Academy family for entrusting me with the leadership mantle for so many years. We worked together to navigate our transition zone and we are now stronger and the future is brighter because of our spirit-filled partnership. You continue to be a Great church, with Great people, serving a GREAT GOD.

To our denomination, the Evangelical Covenant Church, for giving me effective tools to navigate the transition zone with Oakdale Covenant Church.

To my pastor who embodies true excellence and integrity, The Reverend Dr. Calvin O. Butts III, Senior Pastor of the Abyssinian Baptist Church of Harlem, New York. My understanding of the church and its commitment to the community was the result of serving on staff at Abyssinian under your leadership. You gave me my first tools for transitioning a congregation. Thank you for your patience and love.

To our beloved pastor, Dr. Willie B. Jemison, who served as the ultimate change agent for Oakdale Covenant Church for over thirty-five years. The collegiality and support that you shared over the years was instrumental in helping us successfully navigate the Oakdale transition zone.

To the late Dr. Jerry Mosby who introduced me to Oakdale Covenant Church and the Evangelical Covenant Church.

To my beloved Godfather and Pastor, the late Dr. Marke Twain Toles, and Mrs. Minnie Maxine Toles who dedicated me as a baby, baptized me as a youth, and encouraged my spiritual development.

The late Dr. Olen Arrington Jr., who affirmed and shaped my formative years of ministry.

This book is dedicated to all pastors who arrived in the middle of their congregation's movie, continuously persevering in the challenging task of navigating the transition zone.

Rev. Dr. D. Darrell Griffin

ACKNOWLEDGEMENTS

I have never done a single thing of value without the assistance of others. This book is no exception.

Innumerable people over the course of the years have invested in me and actually made this book a reality.

I want to thank Pastor Anthony L. Trufant for his ongoing advice and resources on change and transition.

A special word of thanks to my dear friend, The Reverend Victor Michael Singletary. He believed in the need and value of this particular book. From the outset he has been a source of wisdom, support and encouragement. He went above and beyond the call of duty. He challenged ideas, asked wise questions, and helped to clarify, shape and polish much of the material in this book.

A thousand thanks to my friend and brother, Pastor Darryl Sims, and the staff of MMGI for so patiently answering my never-ending questions about publishing and for shaping this publication in a variety of ways. I will be forever grateful to you for shepherding every element of this project to fruition.

I want to thank Dr. Jocelyn C. Thornton and Pastor Johnna Hayward Muniz for your incredible editing skills and encouragement.

I cannot thank God enough for Pastor Douglas Bixby who encouraged me to write down all of my transitional experiences and stories.

I want to thank Dr. John Wenrich, the Director of Congregation Vitality, for introducing me to ministry coaching through the Evangelical Covenant Church (ECC) and for providing pastors and congregations with some effective tools for transitioning and revitalizing congregations.

Russ Olmon, President of Ministry Advantage, who transformed my life in many ways, not the least of which was calling my attention to the role and importance of coaching and effective systems.

I also want to thank the following people: Dr. Donald Davenport who serves as my pastor in the ECC, Dr. Paul Koptak, my professor who encouraged me to turn my doctoral thesis into a book, Dr. Raphael G. Warnock, Dr. David L. Sutton, Pastor Bryndan Crawford Loritts, Pastor Kevin Davenport, Pastor Melvin Dillard, Pastor Garland Singleton, Reverend David Washington, Reverend Leslie Sanders, Reverend La Brandi Thomas, Reverend Velajo Garrett, Reverend Lawrence Pointer, Pastor Conway Boyce, Pastor Jerome Nelson, Pastor George Wilson and so many others.

Every vibrant ministry has a number of integral people at its core who keep all the people and activities of the ministry connected to its overall mission and purpose. My staff is that invaluable group for me. For years they have faithfully served and played significant roles in transitioning Oakdale: Office staff (Sisters Mary King, Carol Friar, Savona Giles, Delores Humphries, and Vernee Washington) and Church Board Chairs (Harold Gaines, Carolyn Brown, William Pettus, Lynette Lewis, Douglas Brown and Lisa Cardine).

I want to thank the many pastors and churches across the nation who shared their time, experience, and insights with me. Without their help, this project would never have been born. Their assistance is yet another reflection of the church at work, showing a greater spirit of cooperation than competition, and deeper concern for transformation than public credit. May God repay them each a thousand fold for their help.

Rev. Dr. D. Darrell Griffin

TABLE OF CONTENTS

FOREWORD

More than ever in recent history the church needs leaders who understand and have the skills to lead people through transition and change. Few leaders are better qualified with the proven experience and expertise than Reverend Darrell Griffin. He speaks to the challenges, dangers, and strategies to success for any church leader who is serious about succeeding at leading a church into the future.

Reverend Griffin is not only an experienced practitioner of leading churches from tradition to transition but he is also one of the most studied experts in the church world on transitioning churches. He has done his homework making him one of the leading experts on this subject.

Anyone who has had the privilege of knowing and learning from Reverend Griffin knows that he is a master of utilizing numerous communication tools. He captures powerful concepts and communicates them through every day metaphors with whom everyone can identify. When Rev. Griffin talks about how entering into a church is like stepping into a theatre in the middle of the movie, or when he compares the journey of change to being like navigating a GPS, we all instantly understand the concept and remember it.

Rev. Griffin's humility makes his teaching even more compelling than his wealth of knowledge. He is honest and open about the mistakes he has made and lessons he has learned through the school of hard knocks. In fact, I know that one of Darrell's great motivations for writing this book is to help others avoid some of the mistakes he made as he mastered the skills of transition leader.

This book is essential for any Pastor or church leader who is serious about leading their church or ministry through transition. I wish I had known Rev. Griffin when I was in the years of leading my church through the difficult and potentially perilous waters of transition. This work is profound, practical, and thanks to Rev. Griffin's bright mind, positive personality, and writing skills, it is also an interesting and even entertaining book to read.

Russ Olmon
Founding President
Ministry Advantage Coaching

PREFACE

This book is not intended to be a scholarly or scientific work on the method and practices of leadership, but there is much to learn about ministry and the work of the pastor, particularly as it relates to guiding a congregation through times of major transition. The story begins with my arrival in January 2000 as Senior Pastor at Oakdale Evangelical Covenant Church in Chicago, Illinois after the 30-year pastorate of a venerated predecessor. Not surprisingly, anxiety captured the minds of many congregants as they faced the hard reality of the necessity of change but equally desired to retain the best of my colleague's legacy. Uncertainty about the future and Oakdale's identity and mission fueled resistance to my vision and leadership.

Most of the lessons I have learned can be applied to any situation where the church and pastor face the insecurities and uncertainties of change and transition. Herein one shall find the biblically-based methods and relational successes of the Oakdale family, providentially and serendipitously discovered, upon which we built mutual trust and a commitment to the process of change and growth. While I do not suggest that you attempt to replicate our experience in your church setting, I hope you are able, practically and effectively, to apply the enduring biblical lessons, spiritual wisdom, and ministry achievements we gleaned as we transitioned to a new phase of ministry.

In addition to detailing the Oakdale experience, this book includes many practical recommendations that will help any pastor and lay leadership team navigate ministerial, personal, and communal transitional zones. Note that most of the chapter titles reflect practical advice focusing on things you can do in your context. I am confident that the methods and principles that aided us immensely as we discerned God's revelation for our ministry can also work for you.

Please know that my use of masculine pronouns in reference to the pastor is in no way meant to convey that God does not call women to pastoral ministry. It simply reflects my own gender.

Finally, as you read this book and thereby watch the "Oakdale movie," please be reminded that you are getting only the parts of the movie that survived editing and remained after ten years of pastoral zigzagging between successes and failures. I pray this final cut encourages and empowers you as you guide your congregation through the transition zone.

Rev. Dr. D. Darrell Griffin

MAKING THE TURN

An important quote is found on the office door of a colleague: "The bend in the road is not the end of the road, unless you fail to make the turn." Unfortunately, the reality is that for those who cannot or will not make the turn, it *is* the end of the road.

Successful ministry is about making the turn. Successful ministry is about adapting to new situations and circumstances and learning to work with different people; it's about responding to change, including change that we cannot control. As pastors and lay leaders, we cannot remain so comfortable in our current condition that we fail to transition our ministries in ways that conform to God's plan. The truth is that any pastor who assumes that his or her ministry setting can flourish by simply maintaining the status quo is deceived.

Change and transition are non-negotiable, constant realities of life, and as a result, pastors and lay leaders can sometimes miss God's revelation of His "good, pleasing and perfect" will because of the refusal to adjust to rapidly shifting circumstances. The opening quote above declares the necessity of change and transition if pastors and congregations are to realize personal achievement in their ministerial vocations and collective success in fulfilling "The Great Commission."

In his book *Transforming Leadership: Jesus' Way of Creating Vision, Shaping Values, & Empowering Change*, Leighton Ford writes, "Leadership always involves change, moving people from one point to another, from the old way of doing things to the new, from the security in the past to the insecurity in the future."[1] Ford also contends that "to lead is to

---

1 Leighton Ford, *Transforming Leadership: Jesus' Way of Creating Vision, Shaping Values, & Empowering Change* (Downers Grove: InterVarsity Press, 1991) 251.

struggle. In a world such as ours, in history as we know it, to choose the path of leadership is to be on a collision course with conflict."[2]

Thus, leaders do not wait until they see change and transition in progress; they prepare for it. Leaders carefully and painstakingly analyze our pastoral and congregational settings and diligently discern the mood and climate of our congregations. However, in most instances good leadership leads to conflict because most people have a built-in tendency to resist anyone and anything that appears to threaten emotional and relational stability. This individual, internal inclination multiplies within a congregation and inevitably challenges pastoral power. When pastors overlook or underestimate this psychological and political reality, it greatly undermines our ability to lead, particularly in times of transition.

My purpose in writing this book is to provide both perspective and advice on the nature of change and transition while successfully leading a congregation during times of transition. It is to this end that I will draw from my experience of taking the reins from a pastor who had served the church for 30 years. It is also important to remember that while the dynamics of replacing a longtime pastor are unique, the principles and lessons learned apply to anyone entering a new position of ministry.

In this work I also detail my spiritual growth and vocational progress as a leader while navigating my new congregation through the process of transition toward God's direct and providential will for our ministry. Parenthetically, each pastor-congregation partnership that emerges from the mystery of a pastoral call possesses a divinely ordained and unique set of abilities and skills. God majestically pairs pastors and congregations in accordance with His "good, pleasing, and perfect will" because He equips them with special talents for ministry that He does not give to any other combination. Pastors and congregations can possibly miss their unique opportunities to fulfill the "Great Commission" and

---

2   Ford, 251.

expand the kingdom of Christ on earth if they fail to ascertain God's providential and perfect will for their irreplaceable ministry.

At Oakdale Covenant Church, we successfully navigated the hurdles of transition in pastoral leadership, defining and progressing toward our mission and maintaining the dynamic tension of preserving the past while embracing the future. Oakdale Covenant consequently appeals to all generations. We are a multigenerational congregation, poised for success in the technologically advancing and rapidly scientifically progressing 21st century global village. In the words of the prophet Haggai, we expect our future glory to exceed greatly the golden days of our rich and longstanding legacy.[3]

Most of what I will share with you I learned "on the fly." I realized early on that my formal seminary training had not adequately prepared me for leading a new congregation through the steps of transition. A Master of Divinity program teaches current and future pastors to exegete biblical texts as they prepare sermons and plan Sunday worship services. But by and large, seminary education, at least at the time I attended, lacked strategies, methods, and skills to exegete the congregations and communities to which people are called to lead and serve. It is beyond the scope of most seminaries to equip pastors with skills in psychology, conflict management, negotiation, team building, budgeting, strategic planning, vision development, and even transitional preaching, all of which are important to lead effectively during transition. Thus, I was not at first prepared to effectively and systematically develop transitional sermons and strategies to encourage and empower parishioners through major shifts in the life of a congregation. Regrettably, many seminaries prepare pastors with the skills to lead traditional congregations – the "Moses Generation." They do not train pastors for leadership of contemporary, 21st century congregations – the "Joshua Generation."

Further, in my efforts to lead effectively, I (among many other pastors, I presume) was unfairly scrutinized by my congregation because of the moral and ethical lapses of several highly visible national and

---

3   New International Version, Haggai 2:1-9.

international religious leaders who deliberately deceived followers. As a result, many congregations responded by observing their pastors and all religious leaders with greater suspicion. Quite possibly, the moral and ethical shortcomings and character defects of political, corporate, and religious celebrities over the last few decades have solidified a cynical shadow that falls upon anyone in leadership. Consequently, in the eyes of people in the faith community, a good pastor is an exception rather than the norm.

Finally, it is clear that the obstacles to successful ministry are many. This book endeavors to help you overcome some of them, especially as these obstacles affect what I refer to as "transition zone ministry." Some chapters focus on the important dynamics related to congregational change while other chapters focus on leadership and very practical topics such as the importance of knowing your congregation's history and how to form a Transitional Ministry Group. An example of this is found in Chapter 1, which focuses on the challenges facing a pastor who is entering a new ministry situation.

My hope is that the content found here contributes to the goal of helping you and your congregation see the bend in the road that awaits you, to prepare for it with confidence, and to make a successful turn.

CHAPTER 1

STEPPING INTO THE OAKDALE MOVIE

Chances are you have rushed into a movie theatre only to find that, to your great chagrin, the movie has already started. Despite your best laid plans, an inexplicable traffic jam, your significant other who notoriously and irredeemably moves at a snail's pace, a full parking lot, and the misreading of the starting time all conspire to make you late. Whatever the specifics, a moviegoer missing the beginning of a film remains one of life's most frustrating experiences. It is difficult to understand and follow a movie already in progress. We struggle to figure out what happened in the opening scenes and how it affects the plot as well as the role and reactions of the characters.

In many ways, the frustrations of arriving in the middle of a movie capture the challenges and feelings of leading in a time of transition. The person who is expected to provide leadership is also experiencing a major change. Newly appointed pastors enter into individual and collective congregational stories in progress. A congregation already has a history, a story full of complex subplots and a myriad of intriguing and intricate characters. Whether good, bad, or indifferent, a congregation's history is a living screenplay that a pastor reads and experiences as he establishes relationships with his new congregants, who can be likened to cast members.

In essence, answering a pastoral call writes a pastor into a starring role. Understanding the screenplay and entering into the role with the goal of maximizing a church's performance constitute a pastor's first test. Thus, the ability to make this personal and vocational transition, while effectively leading a congregation from its present state to its future ministry, is the "transition zone."

In November 1999, with the affirmation of more than 90 percent of the congregation, I received a call to serve as the Senior Pastor of Oakdale Evangelical Covenant Church in Chicago. I arrived in January 2000 in the middle of the movie telling the story and starring the members of Oakdale Covenant Church. I succeeded a greatly-loved and venerated pastor who had retired after 30 years of faithful and fruitful ministry. The pastor continued to live in the area, and he maintained his connections and relationships with the congregation. As a result, the Oakdale membership greeted my arrival with both excitement and caution.

Interestingly, I soon found my unwritten job description to be successfully and effectively replacing this legendary Pastor Emeritus without superseding his legacy. In my search for understanding within this context and challenge, I compared Oakdale to an iceberg—only 10 percent of the substantive issues were readily visible. The remaining 90 percent, which possesses the potential to kill anyone or anything in its path, lay hidden below the surface. Behind smiling greeters, harmonious music, a beautiful building, and an entry sign that read "All Are Welcome" were questions about mission and vision, pastoral authority, survival of my predecessor's admirable legacy, interpersonal relationships, and intrapersonal challenges. As the newest member of the cast with a very significant role who had not read the screenplay prior to arriving, I had a primary question of my own: "How would I join the cast and enhance the production?"

On the eve of its centennial anniversary, the Oakdale congregation was transitioning toward a new identity and mission. My first day as Senior Pastor was the first Sunday of the New Year: January 2, 2000. I entered a facility that had been built in 1982. Although very well maintained, it was in desperate need of refurbishing. The church office had one computer and a telephone with only three lines.

Seeking to ensure a smooth transition, my predecessor, to my surprise, greeted me as I entered the pastor's study. Usually a member of the Pulpit Committee or church elder performs this ceremonial function on the first day. Nevertheless, we exchanged cordial greetings and had an upbeat and positive encounter. Although he sat at the conference table in the pastor's study, he appeared very much in control. He did not resemble a former pastor who was fully ready to turn over the reins of power to a young successor. I discerned within my spirit that our relationship early on would be testy. An innocent greeting from an unassuming member confirmed my feelings. This man came into the study and said, "Hello, Pastor." The two of us responded simultaneously, leaving an awkwardness hanging in the air as to who was really the pastor. It was most evident to me that my predecessor remained "the Pastor of Oakdale." I was merely on the track that would lead to this distinction. In the early years of my ministry, seasoned pastors advised me that my name being on the marquee did not equate with the authority of the office.

The pastor's study was a large office containing a combination of slightly new and used furniture but no computer. A cursory glance around the room revealed that my predecessor had been in retirement mode for several years. In addition to a parade of congregants who stopped by the study to extend greetings and offer congratulations, six associate ministers were there to offer prayer. (Oakdale maintains the longstanding custom of praying with the pastor before each worship service). During formal introductions, I learned that only one minister had seminary training; two others were attending seminary. Again, awkwardness filled the room as we were trying to read each other's motives. Shortly afterwards, a group of middle-aged deacons joined us for prayer.

As I mounted Oakdale's elevated pulpit with my predecessor sitting adjacent to me, I observed a vibrant, worshipping congregation numbering approximately 400 persons in a facility that could comfortably accommodate twice as many people. The congregation's median age approached sixty, however a few young single adults and young couples stayed, anticipating the appointment of a new pastor.

Additionally, I noticed that this was a very traditional church where the congregation was dressed in their "Sunday best." The deacons were dressed in black suits, the deaconesses were dressed in white dresses, and the organist and choir members were adorned in formal robes. Someone provided me a hymnal so I could participate during congregational songs, and, not surprisingly, the worship style, filled with hymns and a few dated gospel music selections, was as traditional as the congregation's character and decorum. I vividly recall feeling trapped in the 1980s. I could see early on that to attract larger numbers of young adults and young families, Oakdale would have to adopt a more contemporary style of praise and worship.

As I moved to the podium to offer a few introductory remarks, the congregants jumped to their feet and gave me a thunderous round of applause. I could feel the excitement that filled the sanctuary. The people appeared ready for forward progress in ministry. Without question, Oakdale, on that very bright and chilly Sunday morning, was a faith community with great potential to reach people for Christ and to positively impact its surrounding community in service to the Kingdom of God.

Founded in 1902 by Swedish immigrants, Oakdale had become a predominantly African-American congregation. In keeping with the economic and social shifts in many Chicago neighborhoods, the late 1960s brought wholesale racial and cultural changes to the community surrounding Oakdale. Those transitions directly affected Oakdale Covenant Church by dramatically altering the congregation's ethnic makeup. In 1970, Oakdale issued a pastoral call to its first African-American pastor, Reverend Willie B. Jemison. During his tenure of service and leadership, Oakdale grew numerically from 40 to more than 1,000 congregants. This abundant growth created the need for a new facility, built in 1982. Pastor Jemison created more than thirty ministries to educate, empower, and transform Oakdale and its community. The children and youth ministry assured that an excess of 80 percent of Oakdale's youth attended college or trade school. The athletic ministry, which administered several after-school programs, kept numerous adolescents off the streets, thereby helping them to avoid delinquency. Eight years later, in 1990, the considerable decline in the quality of public education in the surrounding community led to the launching of the Oakdale Christian Academy and Child Care Center, and a new educational building was dedicated in 1992. Pastor Jemison considered the establishment of Oakdale Christian Academy and Child Care Center as his greatest legacy to Oakdale and the surrounding community. Today, more than 350 students a year have access to a quality education they could not otherwise afford.

Not surprisingly, Oakdale was undergoing even more transitions as its neighborhood began to struggle with the traditional urban challenges of high unemployment and underemployment, failing schools, intractable violence, and the loss of profitable businesses. Understandably, the flight of businesses worsened unemployment and decreased tax revenues needed to support schools. Regrettably, a once solidly middle class community was now in the throes of inner-city decay. Known for its innovative youth ministry and community outreach in the '70s and '80s, Oakdale at the beginning of this century was becoming an aging congregation with a fragile Children's and Youth Ministry. Historically, Oakdale had not adapted well to changes in membership and community. How would Oakdale Covenant Church respond to such major transitions within and outside its walls?

Not long after I was selected as Pastor Jemison's successor, the Oakdale congregation demonstrated its veneration of Pastor Jemison by bestowing on him the title and honor of "Pastor Emeritus." They further chose to forego a call of an Interim Pastor as they reasoned the Pastor Emeritus could serve in this role as an advisor.

Notwithstanding the other pressing social, economic, and demographic difficulties that Oakdale faced, its transition in pastoral leadership became the most urgent concern. As the new Senior Pastor, I

9

had the task of sensitively implementing new, life-sustaining ministries that addressed the needs of congregants and community residents while simultaneously and diplomatically maintaining a healthy relationship with my predecessor. This balancing act necessitated that I assure the Pastor Emeritus that his ministerial service and personal legacy at Oakdale Covenant Church would be remembered and respected.

In my efforts to juxtapose these competing programmatic and political priorities, I quickly recognized an alarming division within the congregation. The first group enthusiastically advised that we change everything. A second group insisted on preserving the traditions of Oakdale, thereby respecting those persons who had created them and leaving things unchanged. Reconciling these extremes became particularly difficult as a result of individuals floating between the two groups. Their inability to commit to a central direction for our ministry clearly demonstrated how unprepared we were for fluctuations in a transitional zone.

As earlier noted, whereas my seminary education had sufficiently prepared me for Sunday morning worship services and preaching, it had failed to equip me with the necessary tools of practical pastoral ministry during the other six days of the week. I learned to exegete biblical texts, but I did not know how to analyze a congregational setting. My substantial theological training did not transfer into any understanding of human behavior or leading people. I needed skills in team building, conflict resolution, negotiating, and budgeting. As we began the journey of navigating the transitional zone, I quickly accepted that I was unprepared for the myriad challenges we would encounter.

The Need for a New Map

A few years ago my father and I took a road trip to his hometown of Atlanta, Georgia to visit one of his sisters. That lengthy roundtrip drive afforded us some father and son time, which I still treasure in my heart. I drove most of the way, however upon reaching Atlanta's city limits my father decided he would drive while I navigated. Soon I discovered that my aunt's street address and highway exit were not on the map. I said to my father, "Daddy, I don't see Aunt Dot's exit or street address on this map. There is a problem. We need to pull over." My father responded, "What are you saying? It's on the map. I can't believe you graduated from Morehouse College and Harvard Divinity School and you can't read a simple map." He pulled over while lecturing me about my lack of map-reading skills, then said, "Give me the map!" As he took the map, I noticed that it was ten years old. We both laughed and then called my aunt for directions. Our precise problem was our attempt to get to a new place using an old map!

Oakdale and I faced a similar problem as we began ministry together. Inevitably, many pastors in transitioning ministries face the same predicament. Both the leadership and I sought to lead Oakdale to a new place using an old map that did not provide the details necessary to help us navigate through the maze of transition. We needed new directions, a new map, and new skills to prevent aimless wandering as we traveled the difficult road of transition.

On top of everything else, tension among some Oakdale congregants regarding my appointment started to adversely affect the transition process. A small but vocal group doubted the pastoral search committee's selection process. As a result, questions were swirling around the ministry: "Did the pulpit search committee move too quickly in its selection and appointment of a pastor?" "Did they fail to tell us things we should have known?" Using my old map, I tried to reassure the congregation in preaching and teaching that I was indeed God's sovereign and providential choice for Oakdale. But the rising anxiety made it very difficult for them to trust me. I believe that my transitional approach was part of the problem. I approached transitional issues without a clear plan; thus my strategy was unpredictable.

Even a year into my pastorate at Oakdale, there were still high levels of resistance toward my pastoral vision and goals. The need for a new map and a practical paradigm could not have been more evident. The list of enumerated congregational needs and challenges greatly exceeded the resources at my disposal upon my arrival in the middle of Oakdale's movie. I needed practically applicable and pragmatically appropriate methods with clear directions for the transitions we were facing. Questions about pastoral leadership and trust still surfaced: "Will the new pastor do what he says?" "When will the new pastor fully explain his vision for the ministry?" "Is the pastor listening to the needs being articulated by the membership?"

Eventually I learned what I needed to know so that both the Oakdale congregation and I could successfully negotiate the bend in the road. For example, initially I did not organize my preaching to systematically address the leadership, trust, congregational, and personal issues the transition had created. I did not fully appreciate a weekly sermon's potential to minimize transitional stress, nor did I understand that the right kind of preaching could create a tidal wave of changes in a congregation.

Another early realization, also to be explored more completely in later chapters, was the importance of the pastor and leadership team working together to exhibit the right, positive attitude in order to help the congregation move through the peaks and valleys of the transitional period. Defining and implementing new strategies demands unity, if not uniformity, between pastor and lay leadership. Otherwise, the congregation will sense an emerging tension. Accordingly, they will not endorse transition adjustments even if they mentally assent to their necessity. Hence the need to delve a little more deeply into what "transition zone ministry" is all about.

CHAPTER 2
TRANSITION ZONE MINISTRY

Churches (and pastors) arrive in a transition zone in several different ways. As noted, one way is the arrival of a new pastor. However, churches can also find themselves in transition zones when the community changes around them or when new people in the congregation opt for a realignment of ministry priorities. Further, mega trends in the broader culture can also push churches into transition zones. Unfortunately though, many churches that ought to be in a transition zone refuse to change in any meaningful or substantive way in order to remain vital.

I define the "transition zone" as an existential space that separates a congregation's spiritual, emotional, psychological, and missional past from its future. Located at the intersection of a sacred past and a secure future, identity and ministry in the transition zone crucially determine a congregation's destiny. It should be noted, though, that pastors and congregations choose the settings of their transition zones. Will they opt for 40 years of wilderness and wander aimlessly between Egyptian slavery and the prosperity of the Promised Land? Or will they ascend to the Upper Room and await the dawn of Pentecost when the Holy Spirit descends and empowers the apostles to lay the foundation of the early church? Decisions in the transition zone critically establish the relational health and potential of a pastor-congregation partnership to minister internally and externally.

The tragic and horrific events of 9/11 triggered a state of emergency for the United States in terms of air travel safety and security. Our citizens finally understood that the Atlantic Ocean no longer provided the impenetrable border that it did in the World War I and II eras. Because we were attacked from within our borders as a result of lax immigration procedures and air traffic practices, the U.S. government completely revamped these policies and protocols to address the crisis and secure a non-terrorist future. The current state of many distressed American congregations should trigger a similar response in the American Church. Many congregations, on the verge of closing, have a disproportionate number of elderly members. Very few longstanding and historic congregations possess the capacity to reach "Generation X" and the "Millennials" — adolescents who became young adults at the turn of the century. Undoubtedly, a congregation full of senior citizens has a great deal of wisdom but modest flexibility to change. In contrast, a congregation comprised mostly of youth and young adults has a great deal of flexibility to change, but modest wisdom. As neither congregational type can succeed long-term, both face the need to foster a vibrant future for posterity. In each of these transitioning churches, pastors and lay leaders have the monumental responsibility of guiding the congregation through the difficulty of letting go of its uncritical allegiance to the past in order to secure a bright future.

The extremely fragile condition of many American congregations warrants sounding an emergency alarm at fever pitch. Many once strong and flourishing congregations now find themselves on life support, with the impending threat of closing their doors forever. As recent studies from the Hartford Institute for Religion Research confirm, my characterization is not sentimental or melodramatic. Perhaps the demoralization of so many pastors and lay leaders who work tirelessly to prevent the death of churches is the greatest pain of all. Their broken spirits and shattered hearts are the unfortunate outcomes of congregations that fail to embrace the positive potential of ministry in the transition zone. Whether a church is well established with a seasoned pastor or fledgling with a newly appointed pastor, transition zones are inevitable. How a pastor and congregation handle the obstacles and opportunities of this existential space intrinsically defines their future.

As pastors and lay leaders lament loudly because of a perception of aimlessness during the transition zone, it becomes for them a twilight zone where "weird" people now reside and strange things happen. With nostalgia, church leaders wonder where the church has gone. Whether you arrived in the middle of your church's movie a few years ago or 100 years ago, the challenges are greater, the pace is quicker, and the future is more uncertain than ever. The potential for churches to survive, and even thrive, amid a state of crisis and change connects directly to the pastor's and church leaders' effectiveness in identifying and utilizing resources about transition. Admittedly, answering a call to guide an established congregation through a collective transformation to a new ministerial vocation and purpose is not for the faint of heart. This particular challenge in pastoral ministry exists for those pastors who are willing to endure until their congregations and themselves reflect God's purpose and plan at this juncture in their ministry.

The Pastor and the Transition Zone

At some juncture in each pastor's ministry, logging time in the transition zone is both non-negotiable and inevitable. Few issues persistently agitate our faith as much as tension and conflict between pastor and lay leaders when navigating a congregation through the raging waters of transition zone ministry. As the church leadership team shares uncertainty over the process, purpose, and protocol of the church's transition, it puts a tremendous strain on the relationship between pastor and lay leaders. Often an impasse arises from leadership deficiencies of inexperienced, recently installed pastors who circumstantially land in the transition zone without adequate interpersonal and intrapersonal resources to successfully direct the church's transition. This lack of knowledge destroys healthy congregations as they become obsolete. An African proverb states, "When two elephants fight, only the grass suffers." In like fashion, when a pastor and leadership team clash over the direction of the church, the congregation ultimately suffers the greatest loss.

The battles and drama during transition in many churches require both pastors and lay leaders to courageously pick up their crosses and daily crucify their egos and positions of power and influence. They must willingly step out of their religious comfort zones to build genuinely spiritual infrastructures as they successfully guide congregations through the difficult maze of transition. Leading during a "pastoral transition zone" requires the confidence to articulate and pursue a divinely imparted vision for ministry in the midst of an often difficult and anxiety-filled time in the life of a congregation. Whether one is a seasoned pastor or recent seminary graduate, surviving emotional landmines and power struggles is a primary test of leadership. Suffice it to say that, given the challenges facing many congregations today, pastoral transitions can be difficult even in an ideal setting.

Not surprisingly, the excitement of a pastoral call to a congregation, the formal installation ceremony, and the brief honeymoon between pastor and congregants often quickly yield to total frustration. The burden of navigating in a sometimes turbulent environment produces a love-hate dynamic for many pastors in transition. They love a few aspects of their jobs and hate other obligations. Most pastors love preaching, teaching, and leading, but are less enamored with the difficult task of convincing their congregations that transition to a new era of ministry is necessary and worthwhile. When sensitive transition issues surface within the congregation, pastors often feel a strong desire to retreat to their former careers or to explore vocational alternatives. (I thought about returning to selling ceilings and floors in corporate America.)

Many factors contribute to a pastor's success or failure in his or her attempts to navigate a congregation through a transition zone. One major challenge stems from the different ways people understand the role of pastoral ministry and leadership. Typically, the lay leadership team is not united on what is expected of the pastor. This conflict of expectations can be as wide and varied as the many different people who make up a congregation. Satisfying one set of expectations inevitably alienates other views. In an attempt to build a team and cultivate supporters

16

who catch the vision of ministry, pastors in transition indirectly solidify "opponents" who need more time and persuasion.

In addition, the intensity of transition drama rises as congregants misperceive a pastor's ministerial vision. The variance between a congregation's expectation of its pastor and the pastor's understanding of pastoral duties and authority is often great. A pastor may be ready to implement the first few phases of his vision. However, the congregation is unable to follow his leadership and direction because they do not agree, understand, or believe he has the authority to pursue his ministerial vision. Possibly they are still grieving the loss of the previous pastor, especially if he enjoyed a long tenure with them. Further, many congregants may be experiencing serious internal conflicts. Or the congregation might have lost its focus during the pastoral search process, causing many members to feel hopelessly abandoned by God.

Typically, congregations announce they are looking for a pastor "to move the ministry forward," "take us to the next level," or "accomplish the ministry that God has for us today." In many instances, these congregations really want someone who will maintain the status quo. Some churches are looking for spiritual curators who, like administrative directors of a museum, preserve and protect the permanent collection of tradition, ritual, and history. They limit change to a visiting exhibit for a clearly delineated period of time. In church parlance, a visiting minister and choir is as much change as these churches can tolerate. Other churches want someone who will manage and maintain the artifacts of their heritage and legacy by retaining dysfunctional ministries and outdated practices. In this case, pastors are essentially housekeepers who dust off the furniture, clean the floors, and polish the silver. Change is limited to rearranging the furniture after a major meeting to obtain permission to do so.

Serving as a pastor in transition seduces the brightest, most gifted, and experienced clergyman (not to mention the idealistic recent seminarian who just accepted his first pastoral call) into trying to become the perfect pastor. Someone afflicted with this Messiah complex strives to meet all of the expectations and needs of the congregation—individually and collectively. In Pauline terms, the pastor tries to be all things to all people, hoping to earn a 100 percent endorsement of his pastoral vision and authority. This self-imposed pressure of pastors to be all things to all people notwithstanding, some of the congregants' expectations are totally unrealistic. Hence, the idea of a perfect pastor is a fallacy that pastors in transition should strive to avoid. The following humorous item, given to me by a friend, demonstrates the delusion of "The Perfect Pastor:"

"The perfect pastor is one who preaches for 20 minutes and sits down, condemns sin without offending anyone, works 16 hour days doing everything from preaching to sweeping, makes $400 a week and gives $200 back to the church, wears nice clothes, has a model family, supports good causes and helps panhandlers who stop by the church. The pastor is 35, has been preaching for 40 years, and has a burning desire to work with the youth. Yet the pastor spends all his or her time with the senior citizens. The pastor smiles all the while keeping a straight face, because the pastor has a keen sense of humor that finds him or her seriously dedicated. The pastor makes 20 visits a day, spends every waking moment evangelizing, and is always in the office in case someone is in need. The bad news is, the pastor burned out and died at 37."[4]

Longstanding and revered Baptist Pastor Dr. H. Beecher Hicks, Jr., in his book *Preaching through a Storm*, further illustrates the sad reality for pastors who succumb to this unreasonable pressure:

"The pastorate is the worst job you will ever love. Its demands are unreasonable, its calling inescapable, its machinery often unworkable, its concepts difficult to grasp, and the political realities of the work make "success" almost impossible to achieve. We always live with the uneasy knowledge that we are not, and never can be, what others think we are."[5]

---

4 Anonymous, "The Perfect Pastor."
5 Dr. H. Beecher Hicks, Jr., *Preaching Through a Storm* (Grand Rapids: Zondervan, 1987) 11.

Lessons from Seasoned Pastors

In thinking about the advice "seasoned" pastors who successfully navigated a transition zone would offer to novices embarking upon this arduous experience, I recalled a retirement notice, "My Last Lecture," that I received from a former professor. Many colleges and universities maintain a tradition called "The Last Lecture," which allows a retiring professor a final opportunity to give his parting words to the academic community. Applying this tradition to the ecclesiastical world, I asked two seasoned pastors for any wisdom they wish to impart to young pastors.

One of the two pastors I asked was my predecessor, Dr. Willie B. Jemison, who, as noted, retired after thirty years of fruitful ministry at Oakdale. Despite a tenuous start, my lengthy and patient investment yielded a fruitful bond, and our relationship evolved into one of mutual respect and love. Pastor Jemison began by quoting J. Oswald Sanders' book, *Spiritual Leadership*, stating that "often the crowd does not recognize a leader until he has gone, and then they build a monument for him with the stones they threw at him in life." These strong and stinging words were meant to prepare me for the sobering reality that the congregation, in all likelihood, would not fully understand my leadership during my time of service; being misunderstood and underappreciated is a definite part of the pastoral calling.

Second, Pastor Jemison advised that it is difficult for people to grasp the "bigger picture" when they are painting the canvas. Pastors and lay leaders have the panoramic view. They see opportunities and obstacles. However, the majority of the congregation sees only what directly affects them. Pastors and other leaders make decisions for the whole congregation, not individual parts. This is the blessing and burden of a visionary leader. He sees what others cannot see because they lack vision, and he turns his vision into a reality.

I asked a few additional questions during my conversation with Pastor Jemison, including, "How long does a transition take?" After laughing, he responded, "Son, remember transitions can't tell time. It could be in a few years and it could take as long as seven years. One of pastors' and leaders' deepest struggles will be with God's timetable because God's timing doesn't always fit our timeframe. Transition and change seldom happen suddenly. They are the result of many moments, days, and years. Young man, it took me six years before the congregation actually viewed me as their senior pastor. For the first six years, I was the hired hand serving at the whim of a flighty church board." Pastor Jemison's comments were too familiar as I immediately considered my own transition into the role as Pastor of Oakdale Covenant Church. It took an additional year (a total of seven years) before the congregation fully recognized me as Senior Pastor.

Pastor Jemison's final statement was the most impactful. He said, "Son, make sure you leave the ministry in better shape than you found it. And this, my friend, will require taking risks."

As he spoke, my mind drifted to one of my favorite movies, *Indiana Jones and the Last Crusade*. Near the end of the movie, Indiana Jones' actions illustrate the attributes of a genuine leader. Jones passes three supreme tests, reaches the Holy Grail, and saves his dying father's life. Jones' first test, "breath of God," requires him to walk down a corridor and bow precisely at the right moment to prevent revolving metal blades from cutting off his head. In "the Word of God," the second test, Jones walks on the exact stones that spell God's name in Latin to avoid falling through the floor to his death. Advancing to the real test of faith, "the Path of God," Jones nears the edge of a large chasm, 100 feet wide and 1,000 feet deep. On the other side, the doorway to the Holy Grail. He reads these instructions, "Only in the leap from the lion's head will he prove his worth." In assessing this situation, Indiana Jones initially concludes, "It's impossible. Nobody can jump this." But he then realizes that this third and final test requires a leap of faith. His father says to him, "You must believe, boy, you must believe!" With all the faith he can muster, Indiana Jones walks to the cliff's edge, lifts his foot and steps out onto thin air. Meanwhile, he prays fervently that he will not fall into the cavern below. Instead of falling to his death, Jones steps out, and a nearly invisible path holds him up as he walks to the other side. Once Indiana Jones makes it across the invisible pathway, he turns back, throws some dirt across the path, and discovers it is no longer invisible. Herein lies the wisdom regarding the character of a true leader: an effective leader steps out in faith and leaves a trail for other leaders and people to follow.

My mentor and pastor, Dr. Calvin O. Butts, III, Senior Pastor of Abyssinian Baptist Church of Harlem, New York, also offered words of wisdom and counsel. Dr. Butts has had more influence than anyone else on my ministry and leadership style. His transition preaching and leadership during the last 20 years were instrumental in transforming Abyssinian's participation in Harlem, as this urban community progressed from inner city plight to economic revitalization. His inspirational messages motivated individuals to strengthen their faith and rebuild their communities economically, socially, and politically.

I asked Dr. Butts the same question I had posed to Pastor Jemison: "How long does a transition take?" Similarly, Dr. Butts answered, "It will take a lot of time and patience. In fact, transition is a journey and not a destination. Even your changes will change. I will also add there are no shortcuts in transitioning a congregation or community. While there are enhancement and miracle drugs that are used by many to improve their performance, there are no steroids in the work of Christ. God moves at God's own time." He added, "Transition, my brother, is risky business. You could lose everything trying to move a congregation and community forward. However, we are people of faith. We (pastors and leaders) are called by God to be risk takers for the work of the Kingdom. Everything that our churches and communities need is outside of our comfort zone, so we need to be prepared to struggle, and in some cases to fight, to overcome the obstacles along the way."

Dr. Butts' feedback reminded me of a time I stood in the waiting area of a seafood restaurant with some friends. I noticed a large aquarium in the corner and moved closer to observe what was happening inside. To my surprise, I spotted a lobster without its shell. Since I had never

21

seen a lobster without a shell, I found this to be quite unusual, and was even more concerned about the fact that we would be eating there! I thought to myself, "We're supposed to get fresh seafood and that thing looks sick. What's going on here?" I asked the hostess about the sick-looking lobster. She replied, "In order for a lobster to grow, it has to shed its shell. If it doesn't, the shell becomes its tomb." Being a preacher, I thought to myself, "Now that will preach!" A lobster's shell protects it from all predators, but in order to live it has to risk its major protection mechanism. In other words, the lobster has to risk its life in order to grow! What does this mean for us as leaders in transition? Simply this: despite the tough terrain and twists in the road for pastors and leaders, God allows them to progress through the transition zone. Yet, in order to grow, congregations must shed their shells of tradition, history, and legacy. Pastors and congregations need to risk the creation of a new life if they will endure for a future generation. Failure to risk innovation will slowly kill a once thriving ministry.

CHAPTER 3

FORM A TMG
(TRANSITIONAL MINISTRY GROUP)

One of the biggest misconceptions of many pastors is the belief that they are solely responsible for navigating the congregation through the transition zone. This faulty thinking can produce a "Lone Ranger Syndrome" within pastors. The Lone Ranger Syndrome is a term that society uses when a leader has a desire to be far ahead of the group that he or she is leading. This type of leader typically wants to control every aspect of the transition because he or she feels that the transition will fail if he or she is not overseeing everything. The question is, "How can pastors who are lone rangers truly lead if they do not keep contact with the needs of their followers?" Being far out front and shouldering all of the responsibilities may be noble, but if no one is following it can destroy a ministry. I was certainly guilty of this illusion and it produced a "Lone Ranger Syndrome" in me.

Several factors contributed to this misconception. One, I internalized intentional or unintentional statements from some of the pulpit committee members and parishioners who made comments such as, "I really hope that you can turn this church around," "Pastor Griffin, we are counting on you to get us to the Promised Land," "I pray that you are up for the task. Oakdale can be a difficult church to lead," and "Pastor Griffin, you must be careful because the people who have your ear now may not be giving you the right advice."

Another contribution to this misconception was the "trust factor." As a new pastor who inherited staff and key leaders from the previous pastor, I was not sure whom I could trust to give me the right advice and insight for our transition. I was afraid that if I let people into my inner circle, I wouldn't know whether they would really work with me or against my new vision for Oakdale.

Finally, the hurt that contributed the most to my "Lone Ranger Syndrome" or to the "shoulder all of the responsibilities for our transition" mindset, was likely developed during my previous three-year call as Senior Pastor to a different congregation. My first call as Senior Pastor was to a congregation that had a history of unhealthiness and dysfunction. Although we parted ways peacefully, with many expressing their apologies for the congregation's behavior and history, the experience left me with very painful, open wounds that nearly infected my new assignment as pastor of Oakdale.

As I was transitioning to Oakdale, one of my mentors reminded me (and he is still reminding me) to avoid carrying the unhealthy experience of my previous pastorate to my current congregation. But I have come to understand that, unintentionally, I did carry that pain to Oakdale, and that pain produced in me a need to protect myself from anyone who could potentially control or hurt me as my previous ministry did. As a result, my actions were alienating key people who had ideas that could make our transition much smoother. It took me several months of counseling and coaching from mentors to help me uncover and work through my need to control every aspect of our transition. However, I could sense early on that the work was too great and my control tendencies were stifling, neutralizing and stalling the ministry. Pastors must beware of this tendency because many pastors have a controlling spirit that shows up from time to time. Thus, if the Lone Ranger Syndrome and the controlling nature are not addressed, the transition zone will be a long and miserable experience for everyone.

While expressing my transition frustration to a mentor of mine, he suggested that I put together a small task force of members to discuss some of our transitional challenges. I was very reluctant at first because of my need to control the dynamics of our transition and, frankly, I did not want to create another group that had the potential to hinder our already snail's pace transitional process. I was reminded that isolating myself from people who could serve as resources to smooth our journey through the transition zone was an unproductive choice. Many pastors and church leaders fail to understand that what we know collectively can accomplish a lot. Therefore, many pastors do not use their collective congregational resources as well as they should, especially since this requires going outside their comfort zone and sharing power. Further, pastors are distracted by other responsibilities and isolated from those who could teach them a lot about ministry and serve as their greatest support. Pastors must realize that it is only by acting cooperatively in the context of common goals, as the most innovative churches have done, that our accumulated understanding is put to best use. Unfortunately, some pastors see this as an add-on or a distraction from the "real work of ministry."

As I worked through my controlling nature and my Lone Ranger Syndrome, about a year into my new assignment as the pastor of Oakdale, and at the advice of a mentor, I took the risk and put together a small working group whose sole purpose was to provide strategy for assisting with the transition of Oakdale. To my great surprise, I discovered that the wider you cast your net for input during the transition process, the more involved the congregation becomes and the smoother the transition journey.

Arguably, the most important first step toward successful transition zone ministry was the formation of this small working group that later became known as a Transitional Ministry Group (TMG). Naturally, the congregation expects the pastor and seasoned parishioners to lead the transition process, and if we expect success, it is probably best to include as many parishioners as possible. It has been said that the strength of wolf pack, which depends heavily upon the collective strength of the group as opposed to a single wolf, illustrates the necessity of group consent and participation in transition ministry. Indeed, the progress of a congregation on a transition journey relies heavily upon its ability to find unity of mind and purpose in pursuing a new vision and mission.

However, though the pastor resembles the alpha male of a wolf pack, he cannot single-handedly persuade a congregation to accept and implement the vision the Lord imparts to him. Early in my pastorate at Oakdale, I observed some congregants' difficulties with transition to my vision simply because they were not included.

A few years ago, I read an incredible newspaper article detailing an account of a few unemployed fire fighters who started several California bush fires. These firefighters literally started fires in order to have jobs! In reflecting on the story, I saw an analogy with contemporary churches. There are too many unemployed firefighters in the congregation! With nothing to do in a church's ministry, these aimless and disgruntled congregants start brushfires of gossip, negativity, fear, and disunity. Accordingly, pastors and lay leaders need to co-opt this unfocused energy by recruiting these people for a transitional team. Parishioners remain a pastor's greatest asset for transitional and long-term success in ministry. We must remember that people are not pawns for a pastor's programs, but partners in ministry who equally, individually, uniquely, and personally possess divine potential for building the Kingdom of our Lord on earth. Effective and excellent ministry emerges from good, growing, and trustworthy relationships. As I write, I genuinely appreciate many of the members of Oakdale who remain the main characters in Oakdale's movie. Continually, they write the script as the movie unfolds.

Enlisting the participation of a multi-generational cross-section of congregants is an appropriate beginning for a Transitional Ministry Group. This diversity in worldview yields a wealth of perspective on pastoral leadership and personality in addition to many ideas for progressing through the transition zone. Though the expanse of the age range can create a communication chasm, if mined for its true riches, this group contains an incalculable cross-fertilization of techniques for achieving and sustaining the long-term objectives and goals of transition. At Oakdale, this faithful and opinionated group that morphed into the Transitional Ministry Group implemented and evaluated transitional strategies, including sermon development, Bible Study, and congregational meetings.

An atmosphere of openness and positive outlook does not exempt the TMG from the interpersonal difficulties that are inherent in such a group. The difficulties that arise in the TMG require immediate attention and resolution. Beyond seeking cohesion within the variance of opinions and differences among group members, pastors need to lead them toward a unified goal, thereby guarding against loss of focus and change in purpose. To facilitate adherence to our fundamental principles and plans, Oakdale's TMG signed a behavior covenant, both individually and collectively, to maintain respect and trust in the group.

The TMG consisted of twelve congregants, whom I chose, that met every Monday for 90 minutes in eight-week increments. As noted, the group was multi-generational, ranging in age from 17 to 75. I intentionally wanted the TMG to consist of parishioners who were at different places in our transition process, and we enjoyed a mixture of people who supported our transitional process as well as others who were outright against it. This diversity yielded a chorus of different voices at the table guiding our transition process. A personal invitation to serve on the TMG was very powerful, as each participant felt special and welcomed an opportunity to direct Oakdale's transition process. However, we structured the TMG to prevent undue influence from either personality conflicts or any single individual.

At our first TMG gathering, I laid out the purpose which was to gather information regarding the successes and challenges of our transition and to provide a strategic plan for navigating Oakdale's transition. I also informed the church board, leadership, and congregation that the TMG had no authority to circumvent normal governing structures and was strictly serving in an advisory capacity. Our initial meeting was filled with statements about our purpose and ground rules for our time together. I worked very hard to ensure an atmosphere of hospitality so that everyone would feel comfortable to share. We also created a no-holds-barred style in which we modeled an open and receptive attitude.

These sessions helped people overcome their shyness and fear that their ideas or statements regarding my leadership style, my personality, or our transition would be ridiculed, disregarded, or retaliated against.

The Oakdale TMG consulted books and case studies and attended conferences that presented successful methods of pastoral transition. The TMG handbook included our purpose, job descriptions, an agenda for each meeting, and a behavioral covenant. Saturating our meetings with Scripture reading and prayer also minimized conflicts. Actually, there were times when these spiritual disciplines became our agenda and consumed the entire meeting.

Welcoming the opportunity to analyze the joys and pains of the church's transition, each TMG participant usually feels honored to be selected to participate in this significant group. Moreover, TMG participants aid you in discovering important personal attributes (assets and liabilities) as well as dynamics about your relationship with them and their fellow congregants. For example, Oakdale TMG members lovingly helped me realize how little the congregation knew about my personality. In addition, they helped me see the challenges of leading and preaching in the pastoral transition zone. They taught me that I did not fully understand their fears and resistance. Initially, members were reluctant to share their personal concerns, but with compassionate coaching and fervent prayer, some began to share their feelings. Still, other group members remained negative even though everyone agreed we desperately needed a fresh approach. It was important to include some congregational stakeholders who were a little bit "edgy" and perceived by many as negative because it allowed us to identify blind spots and it gave us an opportunity to test emerging transitional strategies with people who might be skeptical. If pastors and church leaders can draw in the edgy and perceived negative people and get them to buy into transitional strategy right from the start, then they will know right away if the strategies are compelling. Eagerly, they contributed to developing sermons and Bible studies for navigating transition. At each TMG gathering, I also facilitated the study of Scripture passages relating to transition and change. The TMG's input and research supplied powerful illustrations, ensuring that each sermon, Bible Study, and congregational gathering contributed to resolving our transitional concerns. Not surprisingly to clergypersons, all TMG members had little appreciation for the amount of time and research required for a qualitative sermon. However, after preparing our first group transition sermon, each TMG member became a loyal supporter of Oakdale's need for change.

Work with your TMG produces a creative partnership in which pastor and congregation stumble upon new ways of listening and imaginative connections. Prior to the formation of the TMG, many congregants felt helpless in the transition zone. But this dynamic and unique partnership gave all of us an opportunity to share our anxieties, expectations, and hopes. More importantly, TMG sessions allowed congregants to hear from the pastor outside the pulpit setting. I forthrightly shared my fears and concerns about leading amidst a large and looming shadow of a beloved retired pastor and an increasingly cautious congregation. Each weekly session became an opportunity for mutual support on our journey through transition. I demonstrated that I was listening and that I felt their sense of helplessness. My vulnerability afforded them an opportunity to express their sincerity in supporting me during this most tenuous period of ministry. Slowly, I became convinced that the best strategy to persuade and lead Oakdale was simply to listen.

I regularly asked, "What are the major issues surfacing in our transition?" and "How can the sermon and Bible Study properly address them?" We created small intimate sessions ("From the Heart of the Pastor") to implement their recommendations. True to their names, these sessions encouraged everyone to share heartfelt concerns. Unscripted and sometimes heated in tone, these forums often became opportunities for crying and witnessing of high-pitched frustrations and loud fears about our pastoral transition. It is impossible to overstate the importance of not taking critical comments personally, but of utilizing these opportunities to create a comfortable setting and mutually respectful environment to garner heartfelt contributions and to build trust. Although the congregation briefly heard from me, most of the time was spent attempting to understand any frustrations of our pastoral transition. Through this experience, I discovered that most people primarily sought assurance that their concerns were being acknowledged.

In summary, a carefully chosen and clearly focused Transitional Ministry Group is an essential ingredient to successful transition ministry that empowers others to fully participate in the transitional process. Pastors and church leaders should not wait until the congregation is in the midst of a full-blown transitional crisis before they decide to act proactively to curtail as many future problems as possible.

CHAPTER 4
LEARN YOUR CHURCH'S HISTORY

The metaphor of arriving in the middle of a movie is used to highlight the importance of knowing what a church has experienced in the past and the implications of the past for the present and future. One could make a case that learning a church's history should take place prior to the forming of a Transitional Ministry Group. I would support that argument as there is never a bad time to learn more about the church's past. However, this chapter comes after the chapter on forming a TMG in order to emphasize that the TMG can go a long way toward helping all those in leadership understand the relevance of the church's history, and that was certainly the case at Oakdale.

I developed a greater respect for Oakdale's convictions, struggles, and joys as I painstakingly learned the congregation's individual, familial, and communal history. Further help in understanding Oakdale's traditions and legacy came through a SWOT (Strengths Weaknesses Opportunities and Threats) analysis of the congregation's contemporary state. I recommend this approach for any church in transition.

The TMG listened to Oakdale's history to grasp the character of congregational life. The following questions comprised a congregational survey designed to ascertain our progress in transition.

1. Rate the progress of our pastoral transition from January 2000.
2. What are your concerns about our pastoral transition?
3. How effective has Pastor Griffin been in helping with Oakdale's transition?

Finally, I did personal due diligence by reading congregational minutes, researching the archives, sharing meals with members, and talking with former Oakdale pastors. These approaches gave me an opportunity to stumble upon both joyful and painful patterns of behavior that could speed the process of transition. Pastors leading transitions stand to gain incredible spiritual and historical insights as they commit to due diligence in assessing their congregations.

One important contribution of the TMG as it relates to understanding a church's history is its insightful identification of the church's "third rail" issues. Regardless of how discerning a new pastor may be, he cannot possibly know the height and depth, breadth and width of lingering congregational issues that are emotionally charged and untouchable, carrying thousands of volts of relational electricity. If a pastor inadvertently touches one of these issues, he may electrocute any transitional progress and unintentionally cause the death of his ministerial vision. As every congregation has a few "third rail" issues, it is incumbent upon members of the Transition Ministry Group to enumerate and contextualize these issues for the pastor. Practically speaking, lay leaders can encourage pastors to stay off the tracks and away from the third rail.

My TMG identified Oakdale's "third rail" issues as our pastor emeritus, the worship service, and the family life center. Other potential "third rail" issues might include relocation to a new facility, renovation of an existing building that holds sentimental value for a large sector of the congregation, or phasing out an obviously defunct and obsolete ministry. Amusingly, something as small as moving the furniture around can become a "third rail" issue. Actually, I know a colleague who lost his vocational and career dream of ascending to the senior bishop's slot of his denomination because he moved the furniture of the recently deceased national presiding bishop and pastor of one of the church's largest congregations out of his office while the mourning period was still very raw. If this pastor had had a TMG with people of sufficient character and courage to assist him in identifying this issue, he would not have made such an obvious mistake resulting in his disappearance into oblivion within his denomination.

A pastor ought to know something about a church's history even before accepting the call, and he should certainly make it a high priority after arriving. Again, the TMG can play a huge role in accelerating the pastor's local church history learning curve.

CHAPTER 5

UNDERSTAND THE DISTINCTION
BETWEEN CHANGE AND TRANSITION

Successful transition zone ministry requires the discovery of a new map for both the pastor and leadership. My first step towards understanding Oakdale's transition zone was learning more about how systematic changes impact a congregation, individually and collectively. Each pastor at this stage of ministry experiences this learning curve.

As an important second step within the transition zone, I had to distinguish between change and transition. Prior to coming to Oakdale, I assumed I had a reasonable grasp of the meaning of these words. My daily usage of the words secured my conclusion that they are synonyms. As a Senior Pastor, hardly a day emerges without my hearing "Pastor, it seems like everything is changing. Our church is not the church that I joined twenty years ago." Or "When are things going to stop changing in our church?" These questions motivated me to find ways to clarify the fundamental difference between change and transition.

Unquestionably, change is possibly life's one constant and non-negotiable factor. The 24-hour news cycle that covers political campaigns, multi-national corporations, worldwide economic fluctuations, and local communities in our global village reports immediate change. From the fall of the "Iron Curtain" and Berlin Wall to the burgeoning democracy movement spreading through the Middle East, the world is changing. The rising percentages of women and people of color who hold publicly elected office reflect considerable changes in the American political landscape. Racial and ethnic mixtures of local neighborhoods show communities are changing. Families are changing, too, as citizens in the United States grapple with the hard reality that four of every ten babies are born to single parents. The decline of many denominations has triggered a number of changes in the church universal. Models of pastoral ministry are being forced to adapt to the trends of popular culture, corporate shifts, and technological advancements. The insistence of many new disciples upon hearing music in church that resembles what they listen to on the radio and internet means that worship services and sacred music are changing, but in many cases not as much as they should. Undeniably, whether personal, national or international, life forces change and transition upon everyone. We live through various cycles of physical and mental change from birth until old age. A value-neutral certainty of human existence, change is necessary to experience the "*summum bonum*"[6] (the good life).

To distinguish between change and transition, I began my research by typing the words into Google. Amazingly, I received more than 120 million hits! That result fortified my conviction that change and transition are two permanent dimensions of life. Further, the permeation of the Internet, making any desired level of information and entertainment accessible with the click of a mouse without traveling to a library or research facility or waiting in line at a theater, has completely and irreversibly revolutionized our lives. Thus, it is necessary for a church to learn how to navigate change and transition effectively. Ignoring or rejecting change and transition puts any congregation at serious risk of decline in vitality or death itself. However, despite the incontrovertible fact that it is a driving force in daily life on personal, national, and international levels, we do not embrace change easily.

Prior to my appointment as Senior Pastor of Oakdale Covenant Church, I thought of change and transition as synonyms. More than a decade later, I consider transition to be more significant than change. The work of William Bridges, author of *Managing Transitions: Making the Most of Change*, heavily informs and influences the shift in my thinking. Bridges defines transition as "the process people go through coming

---

6 "Summum bonum" *Wikipedia,<http://en.wikipedia.org/wiki/Summum_bonum.>*

to terms with a new situation."[7] He describes change as external, the outside effect on an individual or organization. Change can be a matter of choice for the person or institution; likewise external forces can combine to coerce change.[8]

In stark contrast, Bridges characterizes transition as internal. "Change is situational: like the move to a new site or the retirement of the founder. Unlike change, *transition* is psychological."[9] One experiences *change* when a loved one dies (situation). The person's or family's experience of the process of bereavement is *transitional* (psychological). Transition is the individual and congregational attitude and emotional reaction in deciding to accept, adapt, or resist shifts in external circumstances. Transition begins with a realization of different facts and our feelings about a new reality. How do we live different yet fulfilling lives knowing that things will never be the same?

Bridges further argues that "it isn't the changes that do you in, it's the transitions." [10] This distinction between change and transition is important for any pastor entering a ministerial transition zone. Without appreciating this distinction, pastors and lay leaders could potentially implement changes while failing to consider the significant psychological impact their decisions may have on the congregation.

The Three Stages of Change

Bridges offers three helpful stages of change for pastors and congregations in transition: letting go (necessary endings), neutral zones during transitions (wilderness), and starting beginning (commencement).

In the first stage of change, people discover and cultivate the willingness to let go of what they feel is normal, predictable, and comfortable. In the case when a pastor retires or resigns, the end of his tenure produces a wide range of emotions: denial, anxiety, shock,

---

7 William Bridges, *Managing Transitions: Making the Most of Change*, 2nd ed. (Cambridge: Da Capo Press, 2003) 3.
8 Bridges., 3.
9 Bridges., 3.
10 Bridges., 3.

confusion, uncertainty, resentment, sadness, anger, or fear. Some congregants will be genuinely optimistic about the change in pastoral leadership, while others will be noticeably anxious. Whichever occurs, it is important to acknowledge and respect both perspectives as the congregation lets go of the previous pastor's way of doing things.

Additionally, the transition in pastoral leadership inevitably causes many congregants to resist any new directions or initiatives. This denial in turn breeds fear and uncertainty about the future, resulting in an overall decline in ministry activity. Not surprisingly, the collective mental, emotional, and internal resistance to an external change in leadership greatly slows the pace of transition to a "new normal" with the next pastor. The perceived acute loss of familiarity and security seriously impedes the congregation's realization that they have to let go of their current sense of identity if they are to move forward.

In *Revitalizing Congregations*, William O. Avery posits, "A change of pastors causes congregations to re-examine their identity; the event produces a *kairos* moment when churches may be more open to change than during a settled pastorate. Hence, new and exciting paths of ministry can be considered and begun."[11] However, if a pastor serves a congregation longer than a generation, congregants understandably intermingle their church's identity with the pastor and the pastor's ministry. Beyond 25 years with the same leader, most people cannot remember a time when that pastor was not their leader. In some cases, the congregation is less known for being Christ's church than for being the long term pastor's church. When any longstanding minister establishes a church's identity largely around himself, he leaves a transition crisis for his successor.

The second stage of change, the *neutral zone or wilderness period*, is the time of exploration and experimentation between wandering away from the previous pastoral leadership and marching toward the Promised Land of the new pastor's vision. Rightly, many members of

---

11 William O. Avery, *Revitalizing Congregations: Refocusing and Healing Through Transitions* (An Alban Institute Publication: Alban, 2002) 12.

the congregation attempt to reorient themselves to the changes and new direction. Confusion about the future and competing demands of a new leader to establish his imprint combine to overwhelm the congregation. Feeling overloaded by the need to accept change and the natural tendency to resist it, the congregation wonders whether they should step backward, march forward, or simply stand still. The impact of wilderness wandering is inherently negative as congregational life becomes more chaotic and individual members question the traditional method of doing things. As the congregation moves through this stage and takes repeated laps in the wilderness, people become angry and begin to blame each other.

Patient commitment and focus on progress in ministry are the main challenges for pastors and congregations in the second stage of change. The intense emotions of this neutral zone produce undirected energy that will further dislocate people and disrupt growth toward a new vision of ministry. Interestingly, optimism and creativity may surface during this stage. Ripe with unimaginable possibilities, this stage is a time of exploration as the congregation rethinks its identity and purpose. It is critical that pastors and church leaders remain optimistic and continue to provide encouragement to the congregation.

The third stage of change, the commencement period or new beginning, finds people ready to commit to a new direction. Now the congregation possesses an internal security that empowers them to pursue an unfamiliar vision even if they are uncomfortable. Practically speaking, they relax emotionally, cease resisting internally, and begin contributing significantly to actualizing their new era of ministry. Ironically, their newfound comfort with transition may cause impatience for more rapid progress. Yet pastors and lay leaders can maintain hope and a sense of stability within the congregation by strengthening and building trust, good communication, and solid relationships. As the new identity and mission of the congregation glacially emerges, the new beginnings stage transforms the necessity of letting go of the past and harnesses the energy of the wilderness wandering into excitement and expectancy.[12]

The Emotional and Psychological Impact
of Change and Transition

Pastors cannot possibly underestimate the psychological impact of change and transition on a congregation. Fear of the unknown (circumstances, people, and shifting situations to varying degrees) and its related and pervasive anxiety will arise. People will feel burdened by learning new ways of doing ministry or accomplishing their purpose in a new environment. Quite possibly, some will conclude that change requires too much. For example, one day a parishioner stopped by my office to express his heartfelt fears about Pastor Jemison's retirement and my arrival as Senior Pastor. He shared frankly that Pastor Jemison was the only Pastor he and his family had ever known. He wondered if I would be able to understand the unique nature of his family dynamics. Accordingly, pastors have the task of convincing their congregations that, despite their wide range of emotions, the dividends that change yields are worth the investment.

What appears to be confusion and chaos can also be a time of creativity and challenge. Pastors, utilizing innovative strategies and channeling congregational reactions during the second and third stages of change, can determine how well a congregation transitions to a new vision of ministry. A pastor who maximizes positive possibilities creates motivation to take the next step. Thoughts and feelings eventually translate into concrete actions. Encouraging and empowering people to respond with favorable thoughts, positive feelings, and affirmative actions can result in a significant change in both ministry and mission.

The Paradox of Change

Before moving to the next step, it is extremely important to acknowledge the inherently paradoxical nature of change. Sometimes

---

12 Bridges, 4-6

bringing happiness and other times bearing sadness, change is neither good nor bad, but it is unavoidable. Like a day that includes both sunshine and rain, symbolizing joy and pain, change immediately fills the heart with excitement and exuberance while simultaneously causing dread and trepidation. Undeniably, the paradoxes embedded within change offer great opportunities for learning more about our character. At the same time, these incongruities frustrate our attempts to create a stable and predictable life. Without fail, change demands further adjustments just when we finally adapt to a new situation. Simply put, the ironies of change can test the pastor's and congregation's faith in God and their trust of one another.

"The essence of growth is the power to change and the willingness to shoulder the responsibility that comes with it." This anonymous author shares enduring wisdom and reminds pastors and church leaders to embrace change with an open mind by engaging in a process that essentially yields development of our character rather than a successful program; it is the process, not the program, which assists us in successfully handling change. Additionally, in order for pastors to understand how congregations process change, they first need to comprehend intellectually, emotionally, and spiritually how they live through change and move through transition. That assertion prompts me to think of a recent change I experienced and to reflect on what I was thinking and feeling at the time. How did my thoughts and feelings influence my reaction? How did I progress through the change? As successful and effective pastors in transition zones, questions such as these can help us learn to sympathize and even empathize with our congregants' emotions and reactions.

When pastors and church leaders reflect on their past life transitions and how they handled them, they will uncover invaluable first steps in learning about the impact of transitions. Thus, pastors and church leaders should grab pen and paper, draw a line in the middle of the page, and chart good times above the line and difficult times below it. They should record their feelings from some of their life transitions, listing the positive emotions above the line and detailing the negative ones below it. They should ask themselves questions such as, "What turning points helped you recover from the low periods in your life? How did you feel? When did circumstances shift towards a more positive outlook?" As the pastor retrospectively scans the peaks and valleys in his or her own life and answers some of these questions, he or she will uncover some of the psychological implications of transition, revealing several personal strategies that can be used when navigating through a transition zone.

I will share as an example my own personal strategies for navigating transitions. First, I discovered that leading people and organizations inescapably involves negotiating changes, which in turn means making transitions to new principles, policies, and procedures. The interrelationship between leadership, change, and transition go together like a hand in a tailored glove. If changes were unnecessary and avoidable, there would be no need for a leader.

Second, I discovered the incredible mystery and majesty of Almighty God in the midst of changes and transitions. Scripture teaches the immutable, faithful, unchanging and trustworthy character of our Lord. The author of Hebrews 13:8 describes Jesus Christ as "the same yesterday, today and forever." Although God never changes, He paradoxically weaves change into the natural order and within our personal lives to accomplish His redemptive purposes. This discovery is reflected in the Incarnation as it is one of the most unique examples of change. Incredibly, and perhaps incredulously, God transitions from His divine nature into human form to set extraordinary examples for us. Within His earthly journey, Jesus changes careers from a carpenter to a fisher of men. He conducts an itinerant ministry and constantly changes locations; as it is written, "The Son of Man has nowhere to lay His head."[13] He deals with difficult and hurting people who eventually assist His detractors as they perpetually insult and reject Him. The Lord Jesus Christ shows us the possibilities of facing complex changes, surmounting associated challenges, and maintaining balance.

---

13 New International Version, Matthew 8:19-22.

Essentially, Jesus personifies the most expert manager of change and transition.

However, transitions need not be negative. The changing seasons, though they contain potential natural disasters, replenish and maintain life's inherent balance. Cresting and flooding rivers, as well as tornadoes and hurricanes, serve an ecological purpose of recalibration and renewal. In the aftermath of these storms, many people become cynical. They simply do not want to accept the loss of the past. They do not want to rebuild, even though they do not have any alternatives. Transitions in pastoral leadership following a long-serving predecessor parallel the wholesale changes of nature. As leaders, we develop sensitivity to the different emotions and methods of each person as he or she experiences fundamental changes. Admittedly, it is very time-consuming to cultivate and nurture this quality of pastoral compassion, but the investment at this stage of change will be most rewarding in the later sequences of transition.

Third, I discovered that attitude is the primary determinant in the pastoral transition zone. Like a magnet, your attitude can be a source of strength and control during change. Positive attitudes attract positive results; negative attitudes attract negative results. The measure of quality of life is not what happens to you, but how you respond to it. The late Hamilton Jordan, the White House Chief of Staff for former President Jimmy Carter and a 25-year survivor of six different types of cancer, suggested to his fellow patients: "Your attitudes and beliefs are your greatest weapons against cancer." Similarly, as pastors seize control of their attitudes in the transition zone, they possess the capacity to create a roadmap for a successful journey to a new vision and ministry.

Some helpful coping mechanisms for effectiveness in transitions for pastors and congregations

1. **Acknowledge and mourn the pain of the past.** Before you can effectively move to the next stage of your ministry, you need to acknowledge fully the pain of the past. This is especially true when movement to a new era involves a significant loss.

Understandably, it may be difficult to find something noble in a situation that hurt you. Yet I agree wholeheartedly with an anonymous author who convincingly suggests that "pain is the touchstone of all spiritual progress." Rather than reflecting once open and gaping wounds, scars from the pain become reminders of divine and gracious healing.

2. **Maintain faith in yourself.** The many twists and turns of the transition zone can take their toll on one's self-esteem as pastor.

3. **Reassess the facts for greater clarity.** We learned that facts were our friends.

4. **Examine your options.** What are your resources? Which factors can you control? What can you negotiate to accomplish your objectives?

5. **Recognize change in its many dimensions.** Nothing lasts forever regardless of how good or bad it may be. "Nature has never sent a storm that did not end," and we have all heard the saying, "All good things must come to an end." King Solomon, arguably the wisest man in human history, immortally advises, "There is a time for everything and a season for every activity under heaven." Congregations experience less frustration as they accept and manage change rather than desperately clinging to the past.

6. **Detail the components of the present change in the congregation.** As we tend to generalize change, we conceivably overlook the exact implications of change in different areas of our lives. Thus, we should focus on one aspect of change and identify the associated fears the congregation may have. What are they most afraid of losing because of the change? Seek to understand their emotional concerns.

7. **Accept the realities of loss in the process of change.** Admit unconditionally to yourself and the congregation that change, whether positive or negative, means loss of something. The price and extent of the loss may tempt some congregants to propose,

"Better the devils you know than the ones you do not know." This understandable scenario leads us to tolerate unacceptable situations. Oftentimes, beyond paralyzing us, fear motivates us to excuse the inexcusable. Clarifying the necessity of and the rationales behind change lessens the impact of reasonable losses.

8. **Seek valid information.** Congregations will doubt anything positive they hear or see about change, so it is important to research and share reliable data. Record information that assists the pastor and congregation in accepting and adjusting to change. Elicit the help of competent persons who can provide data and present it in a user-friendly way. Ask straightforward questions, remain open to views that may be different from yours, and listen to methodically and intellectually respectable information.

9. **Take action.** Escape "the paralysis of analysis" by proceeding to action. Implement a major kick-off event to gain momentum by taking both physical and mental action toward the new vision of ministry.

10. **Recognize potential dangers embedded in the process of change.** Competing demands from various corners of the congregation and the tendency of pastors to acquiesce to people-pleasing impulses increases the fears of the unknown. Surrendering to these anxieties often results in denial. In contrast, we can move full speed ahead by discovering change and its myriad possibilities. The former danger (surrender to anxieties) essentially undermines the new vision. The latter one (move full speed ahead) ignorantly, and perhaps arrogantly, underestimates the lethal consequences. In recognizing these land mines of transition, pastors and lay leaders equally empower the congregation against succumbing to them. Small yet steady steps forward reliably maintain safe momentum toward the goal.

11. **Make a decision.** A secret part of this process is breaking down "big" decisions into bite-sized chunks. Next, work on them one at a time. By contrast, enthusiastic research results in an embarrassment of riches whose bounty overwhelms its possessor. To avoid analysis paralysis, set an inviolate deadline for decision-making. Do whatever is necessary, even if it means flipping a coin or pulling straws, to meet your schedule of timely decisions.

12. **Identify the benefits of change.** For a generation of church members who listen to secular songs entitled "What have you done for me lately?" it is necessary to detail the great gifts provided by change and transition. Every experience contains spiritual and personal lessons. We need only look for them. Helping the congregation understand the tangible benefits of change and transition is a central task of the TMG.

13. **Identify a change partner.** As iron sharpens iron, people who are similarly situated in life encourage and empower one another as they pursue their dreams and goals or face adversities and challenges. Personally and professionally, securing a change partner who commits to running this marathon with you makes the experience less frightening and quickens the pace. A ministry coach (such as www.ministryadvantage.org.) or spiritual director is an ideal candidate. Choose someone who holds a mirror to your face to reflect your fears alongside your highest goals. Your change partner may also be a clergy colleague who knows you well enough to help you see three sides of every situation.

Transition crucibles offer critical opportunities for human and ministry development.

Like various animals that must shed their skin in order to survive or suffer the loss of a part of their anatomy to regenerate and thrive, congregants (and congregations as a whole) embrace difficulties of change and transition, especially if they intend to leave a legacy for posterity. The real hazard they face is the unwillingness to let go of the past. In the natural world, any animal that refuses to shed its skin or accept the losses of the regenerative process transforms its old skin into a tomb rather than a protective shield. Similarly, churches that refuse to let go of their traditions eventually discover that inscriptions on monuments of adoration and proclamations of great historical deeds are actually engraved epitaphs and obituaries. Thankfully, the transition process offers an alternative—a template for understanding stages of personal change.

Finally, it is important that we do not make sacred cows of the changes we implement today. As change remains a constant dimension in any personal or institutional life, a change that was right at one time does not remain the right and best means of ministry indefinitely. Later on, the importance of spiritual formation in the process of transition will be addressed. Suffice it for now to say that as pastors and leaders, we need to be renewed daily. Regularly practicing spiritual disciplines will help provide the strength and courage we need to discard once new techniques as they become old so that the Holy Spirit can lead us to welcome more changes.

CHAPTER 6

CHOOSE YOUR LEADERS WISELY

Phil Jackson, former coach of the Chicago Bulls and Los Angeles Lakers, earned the distinction as one of the greatest coaches in NBA history according to many fans, announcers, pundits, and writers. In the years spanning 1989 through 1998, the Chicago Bulls won six NBA titles. Subsequently, the Los Angeles Lakers won five NBA titles from 2000 to 2010. Breaking the previous record of nine championship wins set by Red Auerbach, Jackson has eleven NBA titles as a coach. How did Jackson manage to consistently motivate such famous and divergent teams to win? His ability to harness a seemingly limitless number of egos (including diverse players and their agents) to earn multiple titles simply amazes me. Arguably, Jackson has led the most dissimilar and egomaniacal teams in recent NBA history. Somehow Jackson was able to get them to buy into the team concept. Bewildering to outside observers, he enabled his teams to grasp the ultimate goal of winning a championship and work collaboratively to achieve it.

A team is a group of people or animals who share a common purpose.[14] The collaboration and synergy of a sports team can be infectious. Actually, it is miraculous to watch each player subordinate his ambitions for records and desire for celebrity status to contribute to the team's cause of winning. Single team members understand the importance of their position and how it affects overall team effort. Teamwork's collaborative exchange maximizes personal strengths and minimizes collective weaknesses. Not surprisingly, Jackson's coaching experiences in Chicago and Los Angeles offer pastors in transition

---

14 "Team." *Merriam-Webster's Collegiate Dictionary.* 10th Ed. 2001.

some very helpful methods to apply within the unique contexts of their church settings.

As we formulated Oakdale's transitional leadership team, I struggled with how to translate for our leadership team some of Phil Jackson's techniques for unifying a team with a compelling and singular goal to an NBA championship. Instead of a priceless ring for each member of the championship team after winning the best of seven games in the finals, we seek the grand and ultimate championship of winning souls for Christ, for which faithful congregants will wear crowns of righteousness throughout eternity.

To this end, we soon discovered that building a team is just as important as casting a vision. Primarily, I learned that a mismatch between personalities and skills amongst lay leaders could spark a crisis that, if sufficiently severe, would threaten congregational stability. Perhaps you are aware of congregations that experienced such crises due to the failure to synchronize these two critical attributes amongst lay leaders. Based on the work of Jim Collins, a business school professor and author of the bestselling book *Good to Great*, Thomas S. Rainer's text, *Breakout Churches*, proved to be an invaluable resource in our journey toward team-building and expansion.

Organizations striving to progress from good to great consider an important principle Collins calls the "who" before the "what." He states, "You have to decide where you are going, how you are going to get there, and who is going with you. Leaders of companies that go from good to great do not start with "where" but with "whom." They start by getting the right people on the bus, the wrong people off the bus, and the right people in the right seats and then they chart their route."[15]

We encountered additional frustration when seeking to find and attract willing and talented individuals to assist Oakdale in moving toward a fruitful future. Prior leadership accomplishments in the corporate sector and secular world did not easily translate into success

---

15 Thom S. Rainer, *Breakout Churches* (Grand Rapids, MI: Zondervan, 2005) 91.

within the ecclesiastical community. Though the structures are very similar, congregations are unique organizations that do not always function in the same manner as corporations or not-for-profit entities. For example, there are behaviors and actions from volunteers in churches that would be totally unacceptable in corporate settings. Among them are tardiness, the demand for responsibility without accountability, and leadership without any training or retraining. In contrast, the corporate sector rarely gives the proverbial "benefit of the doubt" to someone whose standards of professionalism and productivity do not warrant superlative description. In essence, the values of church and corporate cultures clash straightforwardly with regard to use of resources and selection of workers. Therefore, we struggled with getting the right people on our bus in the right seat, and it was very difficult to get the wrong people off the bus. I faced the hard reality that the team we inherited was incapable of transitioning Oakdale to her burgeoning and promising future. The "old guard" did not have requisite skills, was way too resistant, and was simply unwilling to change.

Again, it was difficult identifying, attracting, and retaining individuals to serve. Previously, I restricted team-building skills to selecting persons willing to serve. This approach attracted congregants eager to speed the pace of transition but without possessing the gifts and skills necessary to achieve our aims. Equally challenging was removing team members who were not a fit with other members of the team. Building an effective team was harder than I expected as I assessed the assets and liabilities of the current leadership team specifically and those of the congregation in general. Discerning the right persons with suitable character, chemistry, gifts, and commitment proved to be almost impossible.

This selection process critically determines success in the transition zone. People have an inbred tendency to gravitate toward people who are like them. Failure and confusion result when people are made to relate to people whom they find too dissimilar. To alleviate this potentially costly mistake, Bill Hybels, Senior Pastor of Willow Creek Community

Church and author of *Courageous Leadership*, suggests that the first step in building a dream team is defining its purpose with ruthless specificity.[16] Detail the parameters of the team's work by surrounding its purpose and stick to these practical goals!

The specific purpose in turn establishes clear criteria for selection of team members.[17] What personality and gifts does each position require? This significant question necessitates prioritizing certain qualities based on their importance to the team. Hybels recommends the "three C's" in selecting prospective team members: character, competence, and chemistry.

The personality chemistry and relational dynamic between the pastor and lay leaders can either ease the challenges of a transition or severely hinder its progress. I made the major mistake of assuming that what motivates me also motivates others. Such an assumption has the potential to create a ministry that appeals only to pastors. Gaining interest, consent, and ideas of the people we lead is crucial to a transition's eventual success.

Using the Enneagram

Fortunately, I realized I did not have to be a Phil Jackson clone to acquire skills in building and leading high performing teams within a church. The field of Emotional Intelligence (EI) provides helpful clues in assessing an individual's leadership skills and determining how personality shapes decision making. Personal EI measures a person's emotional intelligence, leadership potential, and interaction with other team members. Two factors comprise emotional intelligence: (1) Intrapersonal intelligence, knowledge and acceptance of oneself and (2) Interpersonal intelligence, effective interaction with other people.

As we were searching for tools to assist in building our leadership teams to navigate the transition zone, I recommended the popular personality assessment tool, Myers-Briggs. It asks a series of questions

---

16 Bill Hybels, *Courageous Leadership* (Grand Rapids, MI: Zondervan, 2002) 80.
17 Hybels, 81.

designed to measure a person's psychological preferences regarding how they perceive the world and make decisions. Many organizations use this assessment tool and others such as Leading From Your Strengths, DISC (a quadrant behavioral model), and Strength Finders to understand the personality traits of their employees. However, the leadership of Oakdale was firmly against using any corporate assessment models in our ministry. They insisted we find assessment tools and models that were biblically based.

Our research turned up only a few such tools that were in line with our conservative beliefs. One of the EI tools with roots in the life of the church is the Enneagram. This 2500-year-old personality assessment tool proved to be an invaluable EI tool and guide as we formed our ministry team. Serendipitously, I learned of this powerful resource during my formal training to become a certified spiritual director. Many spiritual direction programs utilize the Enneagram; it has emerged as a wonderful tool for building teams and strengthening relationships.

The word "Enneagram" sounds exotic, but it refers to a system that categorizes people into nine personality types. According to Dr. Jerome Wagner, author of several popular books on the Enneagram and the International Enneagram Association, the name "Enneagram" means "drawing of nine" and comes from the two Greek words: *ennea* meaning "nine" and *gram* meaning "drawing" or "point figure." The Enneagram is a nine-pointed figure inscribed in a circle. The meaning of the symbol itself coveys a system of knowledge about nine distinct but interrelated personality types, or nine ways of seeing and experiencing the world.

Dr. Wagner further states that "these paradigms or world views become the organizing assumptions and core beliefs that influence and determine our perceptions, thoughts, feelings, and behaviors. They are at the core of how we think and feel about ourselves, about other people, and about the kinds of interactions we can imagine and allow ourselves to have with others."[18]

---

18 Jerome P. Wagner, The Enneagram Spectrum of Personality Styles Training and Certification Program, 2007.

According to those who have done extensive research and studies on the Enneagram, these nine inherent and inalterable personality types are present in any human organism. For pastors and church leaders who seek to understand their congregation's personality, the Enneagram provides a tool for gathering insightful personality information on the congregation and how these personalities possibly interact in group settings and leadership positions. Having access to a congregant's personality profile and behavior in group settings and leadership positions was essential for navigating the transition zone of Oakdale. The Enneagram helped us manage and lead the many different personalities through our transition.

Additionally, as a leader it is vital to know your own personality type in order to understand how other people may respond to your leadership style and personality. When we are functioning from our healthy personality type, our values and vision are clear and our problem-solving capacities optimal. When we operate from an unhealthy personality, our values are conflicted, our vision is narrow and opaque, and our actions are impulsive, compulsive, scattered, and less effective. The Enneagram is a useful tool for understanding both the "upside" and "downside" of our personality styles.

Let us look at all nine types and the word associated with each type:

Type 1 – Good
Type 2 – Loving
Type 3 – Efficient
Type 4 – Original
Type 5 – Wise
Type 6 – Loyal
Type 7 – Joyful
Type 8 – Powerful
Type 9 – Peaceful

According to Wagner, these nine words equally describe an aspect of God's character. For example, God is good — He gives us what we need. God loves — for God so loved the world that He gave His only begotten Son.[19] God is efficient — He does all things well (God spoke and created the world; there is nothing more efficient than that). God is original -before there was anything, there was God. He is wise — He can solve any problem. Loyal — God is faithful even when we are not. Joyful — God is full of joy and He gives us joy. Powerful — He holds all power in His hands. Peaceful — He is peace in the midst of the storm. God is all these things in wholeness and perfection. As we are made in the image of God, each of us possesses a measure of all nine qualities.

We introduced the Enneagram to the congregation at our Wednesday evening service, and I spent nine weeks teaching about the Enneagram and its potential impact for our ministry. Since I was able to teach the Enneagram from a biblical perspective, the leadership and congregation fully embraced it as a necessary assessment tool for moving us forward. In fact, the Enneagram is the perfect tool to use in marriage counseling and many other settings.

Another benefit of the Enneagram assessment tool when in transition is that it fosters better interpersonal relationships, assisting us in understanding what motivates us and others. Miscommunication, misinterpretation, and tremendous emotional pain often result when people assume others should see the world as they do. When pastors and church leaders in the transition zone learn to appreciate how each personality type views, reasons, and explains an identical experience differently, it supplies direction for personal maturity and enriching relationships with others. Through this process I discovered that my personality type is seven, a joyful person. According to Ginger Lapid-Bogda, author of *What Type of Leader Are You?: Using the Enneagram System to Identify and Grow Your Leadership Strengths and Achieve Maximum Success*, persons who are sevens on the Enneagram are typically visionaries. "They are big picture leaders who can emphasize vision

19 John 3:16.

and team culture, however, sevens as leaders often underemphasize team description and process. It is not that they purposely ignore these areas, but simply that they themselves prefer to work in under organized teams. To sevens, too much structure or process restricts their freedom of thinking and movement. While this relaxed organizational style may work well for some team members, others may require more structural and process guidance."[20] This information was critical for navigating the transition zone because it forced me to move out of my comfort zone and push for more structure and process around some of our key transitional initiatives. Although I felt paying too much attention to process and structure was slowing our transition down, many of our leaders and parishioners desperately needed a slower pace and more detail in order to get on board with the new direction. This self-disclosure and revelation equipped me to recognize my family and the church staff with clarity and acuity.

The Enneagram is a powerful tool for communication and creative teamwork, and is now an essential learning tool for both my staff and congregation to improve our leadership placement and development. It is also a great aid for self-understanding and seeing our own habits and ways of thinking, feeling, and behaving. As we become more aware through self-observation, we are better able to make empowering, conscious choices, as they relate to building an effective transition team.

Good leaders appreciate characteristics of different personalities beyond just tolerating them. Transition requires a number of personalities and processes for making decisions. As we approach problem solving and decision making, each of us follows a procedure heavily influenced by our personality type. A wise leader recognizes and embraces the advantage of having different personality types on a transition team. Multiple talents that complement one another uncover many facets of a single issue that one or two personality types might overlook.

---

20 Ginger Lapid-Bogda, Ph.D., *What Type of Leader Are You?: Using the Enneagram System to Identify and Grow Your Leadership Strengths and Achieve Maximum Success* (New York: McGraw-Hill, 2007) 205.

On the other hand, personality differences are potential sources of conflict rather than enrichments. Pastors seeking to stimulate a transition team need to focus on personal motivating factors. What motivates the leaders? What will motivate congregants you may ask to join in transition? What will motivate those lay persons who will implement transitional plans?

A further advantage of using the Enneagram is the insight it provides into how each team member is "wired." This vital information helps everyone else understand the reasons that underlie a particular personality style and offers some explanation of why people behave as they do.

Finally, there is a three-fold benefit to pastors and lay leaders utilizing the Enneagram in transition: (1) a more comprehensive understanding of personal choices and behaviors, 2) a more generous and objective understanding of fellow team members, and 3) a greater possibility to work cooperatively and collaboratively.

This deeper and more detailed self-understanding yields specific insights relating to personal strengths, developmental challenges, and motivations. You gain concrete examples of easy tasks, changes that require work and challenges that always might be a struggle. Fueled with a perpetual sense of urgency about accomplishing tasks quickly combined with little flexibility or empathy, you may not consider how your actions affect others. Yet personal assessment information assists you in evaluating when situations require consensus and cooperation. You will then work on being more patient and open-minded with others and yourself.

Knowing the strengths and limitations of each team member allows everyone to function at a higher level. Each person then knows how he or she can support the whole team. Team members compensate for one another's incapacities. Individuals soon begin to think as a team, desiring to know their colleagues better and identifying ways to help them in order to succeed collectively. I found that the Enneagram has taught us how to function as the Body of Christ as Paul discussed in 1 Corinthians 12.

However, you should be aware that persons who lack self-assertion may appear indifferent initially. For example, some people may say they are "somewhat standoffish" because they lack self-confidence or are skeptical of other people's intentions. Quite simply, they may prefer one-on-one interactions to group activities; they may also be independent. Being perceived as unsocial could be due to any combination of factors, but knowing why someone chooses to be a "loner" enables other team members to relate and communicate more effectively, and they supply insight for developing leadership capabilities and skills.

Let me offer a final example of how we used the Enneagram that you may find helpful. As we entered the beginning stages of renovating Oakdale's sanctuary, I recommended we use the Enneagram for selecting renovation committee members. My suggestion was met with some reluctance. Nevertheless, they agreed to test the Enneagram's effectiveness by selecting individuals that had the One, Three, Four, Five, or Seven personality types. This combination of human chemistry ideally fit Oakdale's collective character. The type Ones, perfectionists and high achievers, ensured the building design plans and construction were excellent and flawless. The Threes, who operate in a system of order, made sure the contractors adhered to schedules. The Fours, inherently creative, pushed to incorporate the latest technological advances of high quality sound and video. The Fives, who are wise and long-term thinkers, waded through our plans to consider future growth and development. The Sevens, enamored by the big picture, enlarged our outlook to attract the interest and involvement of the entire congregation.

At the renovation's completion, the sanctuary exceeded our expectations, and we controlled costs. The final invoice was $85,000 under budget. These achievements in aesthetics and finances eliminated the previous suspicion within our church regarding the benefits of the Enneagram. Following their efforts, the church council and the congregation were fully convinced of the Enneagram's usefulness and how it can help pull together the right personality combinations for completing a task, whether during transition or not.

Whether your congregation uses the Enneagram, Myers-Briggs, Leading From Your Strengths, or some other personality assessment tool, know that these tools can help pastors and church leaders to understand and accept themselves at a very deep level and give insight for developing our leadership capabilities and forming team dynamics. Assessment tools of some kind are necessary for building teams to navigate the transition zone.

CHAPTER 7

BECOME A GPS LEADER
(GOD'S POSITIONING SYSTEM)

Global Positioning System or (GPS) is a satellite-based navigation system that provides invaluable information to persons who have lost their way. The GPS transcends time, space, and weather to supply reliable directions and location anywhere on earth.[21] Recently, I purchased a GPS device because I grew weary of Map Quest searches and printouts that sometimes would not get me to my destination.

After my initial use of the GPS device, I was fascinated and hooked. It seems the device knows more about my community's geography than I do! With each entry of a specific address, the system gives me options of whether I wish to avoid highways, intersections or traffic congestion. It also asks if I want to travel scenic routes or use toll roads. Exquisitely, the possibilities for mapping a route to any destination seem infinite.

One day while driving I decided to test the device's accuracy by turning purposely in the opposite direction of the instructions. Immediately, the device recalculated an alternative route to get me to the same destination. Suddenly, an interesting thought occurred to me. Wouldn't it be great if churches had spiritual GPS devices to determine their next move and calculate the best means of fulfilling God's will with few detours and roadblocks? Actually, God provides the most powerful GPS system in the Person of the Holy Spirit! John 16:13 says, "But when He, the Spirit of Truth, comes, he will guide you into all truth. He will not speak on his own, he will speak only what He hears, and He will tell

---

21 "Global Positioning System (GPS)." *Merriam-Webster's Collegiate Dictionary*. 10th Ed. 2001.

you what is yet to come."[22] Using God's Positioning System is critical for navigating transition zones. Most pastors and leaders are underutilizing or ignoring the critical role the spiritual GPS, or the Holy Spirit, plays in discerning direction for navigating the transition zone. The number of wrong turns, dead ends, detours that can occur on the transition journey requires that pastors and church leaders rely on something much more powerful than their own skills and intellect.

In fact, I would argue that it is necessary for pastors and church leaders to use the spiritual GPS system as the first step towards discerning God's positioning and direction for any congregation's future. This leads me back to my GPS analogy. What I have discovered about the GPS unit that I purchased was that it had a warning that flashed across the screen. It stated, "Do not enter any information while the vehicle is in motion." I found the statement annoying and even time-consuming, but necessary for my safety. As pastors and church leaders set the course for their ministries, few are willing to slow down and bring their transition to a complete stop long enough to allow the Holy Spirit to speak wisdom, direction, and life to their transition journey. Pastors and church leaders must understand that moving forward without fully consulting God will result in a rocky and tumultuous transition journey. With this spiritual guidance, any church can achieve the ministry that God ordains for them.

Wanted: GPS Leaders!

The fragile condition of many contemporary congregations creates a crisis in both pastoral and lay leadership. The resulting turmoil and confusion causes many once strong and healthy churches to consider closing their doors forever. The cumulative pain breaks the hearts and spirits of many pastors and church leaders. Simply put, a fierce leadership crisis exists within many of our churches.

"There always appears to be a dearth of people who are willing to take responsibility, get out front and lead the way. It seems there are

22 New International Version, John 16:13.

many more called by God to lead than respond to that call. The primary reason for this 'duck and cover' syndrome is that leadership is difficult. We would rather take the easy way. After all, leaders are targets for criticism. It is much easier to tell others what they are doing wrong than to step forward yourself. Leadership requires responsibility, bearing the decision-making burdens and carrying the welfare of others."[23]

Congregations living in transition need courageous and proactive leaders who are willing to implement their Transition Ministry Group's action plans. Poor leadership is the routine cause of many problems in the transition zone. Indeed, it is necessary to have leaders who recognize the need to change, but it is quite another challenge to find leaders who possess the requisite character to guide a congregation toward its future ministry. Therefore, pastors and lay leaders must create mechanisms and criteria for selecting, empowering, and encouraging leaders who will forthrightly navigate transition zones.

A self-assessment is an important primary step in determining suitability for leadership. In evaluating whether a person possesses the attributes and skills to participate in navigating the congregation through a transition zone, one must be willing to ask and honestly answer where he or she fits, what he or she can contribute, and explain how his or her contributions influence and expand the transition. Confusion about any of these matters inevitably produces problems during a congregation's period of transition. As leaders attuned to God's Positioning System they must make every effort to assist fellow team members in articulating their roles in fulfilling the vision. As team members buy into the vision of future ministry and clearly understand their respective roles, they will make valuable contributions.

At Oakdale we created "GPS Leaders." These distinctively individual leaders resemble the children of Issachar, who in 1 Chronicles 12:32 are men (and women) who have a keen understanding of the era in which they live; they resolve what Israel should do. The children of

---

23 Greg Ogden and Daniel Meyer, *Leadership Essentials: Shaping Vision, Multiplying Influence, Defining Character* (Downers Grove: InterVarsity Press, 2007) 135.

Issachar were a part of the group that was formed to consecrate David as King of Israel. They had the mission of observing, listening, and ultimately 'discerning the time,' for this grand occasion. They were to know God's will for His people at any given time. Likewise, "GPS Leaders" are spiritually discerning men and women who seek divine guidance regarding a congregation's next moves. They interpret God's written word by recognizing the significance of past events and applying these lessons to present and future ministry.

I would argue that any congregation experiencing transition must prioritize creating "GPS Leaders." The volume of critical decisions that emerges within transition zones demands leaders of this caliber. Arguably, the competing demands of popular culture, rapidly advancing technology, and religious and cultural pluralism in which today's church ministers force tougher decisions on pastors and lay leaders than was the case in previous generations. This reality heightens the importance of discerning God's definitive purpose for congregations. GPS Leaders are the rudders that guide the ship through treacherous and raging waters.

GPS Leaders need to possess many characteristics to navigate effectively in transition zones. Below are a few of those characteristics that time and experience have revealed to me.

GPS Leaders:

1. ...are mission-minded leaders who are focused on equipping the church to reach an ever-changing world.

2. ...adapt to adversity. While many people run from adversity, GPS leaders expect it and are prepared to handle it when it happens. Wherever change and progress are underway, competing interests inevitably rise to challenge them. At that point, leaders must decide whether they will accept the challenge and overcome it, or turn and let their opponents set the agenda.

3. ...are life learners taking the lead in and responsibility for their own learning. At Oakdale a group was developed called the Church Full of Leaders (CFOL). The task of the CFOL was to

connect new or potential leaders to the leadership vision of Oakdale so they could play a critical role in advancing the mission of Oakdale in our sphere of influence.[24] The Oakdale CFOL training program was developed to provide leadership training for new and potential leaders with the aim of developing a strong core of leaders at every level of our church

4. ...possess the ability to display an appreciation for the past and affinity for the future. GPS Leaders build a bridge between the heritage and the future instead of walls that close some in while locking others out.

5. ...fully understand that you cannot get to a new place using an old map.

6. ...know that change is paradoxical.

7. ...know that one of the best ways to learn about transition and its impact is to reflect on their own life events and how they handled them.

8. ...know that God is in the change and transition business.

9. ...seek valid information by writing down the information that is needed and determining who can provide the data.

10. ...recognize that things do change. They accept change and choose to manage it, rather than desperately trying to cling to the way things used to be.

11. ...pinpoint specific change. They are aware that the congregation can do anything, but not necessarily everything.

12. ...are decision-makers, even when all the gathered information seems overwhelming. To avoid analysis paralysis, GPS Leaders set deadlines for making decisions and do whatever it takes to make the change happen, even if the decision must be adjusted later in the process.

---

24 This innovative concept was created and designed by Dr. Jeanne Porter of the TransPorter Consulting Group, a ministry-focused consulting firm. It equipped Oakdale leaders with the competencies necessary to lead according to the mission and vision of Oakdale. All new leaders must complete the CFOL Leadership course in order to assume leadership responsibilities.

13. …know they must maintain a strong devotional life to ensure personal integrity. Transitioning a ministry is very challenging, so daily spiritual disciplines are essential to surviving in the transition zone.

14. …identify change partners. Because change is a constant in today's society, they will go through it many times in many situations. It is important to have change partners, especially ones who have successfully navigated a transition zone. Their encouragement and support will make the transition zone experience less scary.

Finally, "GPS Leaders" and congregations must form a cohesive unit. This partnership needs to embody an invaluable collaboration that successfully navigates the congregation's transition. Any achievements toward a new vision of ministry depend heavily on unity in pastoral and lay leadership. Consider the "V" formation in which geese fly. The annual migratory trips to warmer climates require unity. Flying in formation increases geese flight range by 71 percent. Flapping wings create airwaves that provide uplift for the next bird in formation, thereby supporting it, decreasing its work load, and allowing conservation of its energy. A lone goose could not complete the trip, but in formation, old, young, and even weak geese reach the migratory destination. Simply put, a flock of geese can attain collectively what a single goose cannot. This illustration from nature instructs pastors and lay leaders to strive for cooperative leadership, which encourages and empowers everyone. We are the Body of Christ, created to function in concert with all parts. "The eye cannot say to the hand, 'I don't need you!' And the head cannot say to the feet, 'I don't need you!'" (1 Cor. 12:21). Occasionally, a disoriented or overconfident goose lapses into autopilot and finds itself adrift from the formation. Soon thereafter, its wings become heavy from exhaustion and it loses altitude. It experiences the burden of increasing wind resistance. Then it pulls its weakened body back into formation. In like fashion, pastors and lay leaders cannot disregard the importance of achieving unity by drifting away into a "Lone Ranger" mentality and ministry.

CHAPTER 8
BECOME A "GPS PASTOR"

As mentioned previously, the turbulent and impatient contemporary times in the life of the church, particularly during a transition of pastoral leadership, result in pastoral leadership challenges. These ideological, political, and social trends erode the traditional reverence and deference once given to pastors. Previous generations empowered a pastor with authority to lead a congregation through the intricacies of transition. Today's pastoral leaders are subject to micro-managing from church councils, elders, and other lay leaders. Rigorous "strict scrutiny" eliminates any possibility of strong, proactive leadership.

However, pastors assume a proprietary share of accountability and responsibility for leadership in the transition zone even if they have been divested of the necessary authority to succeed. Not surprisingly, the challenge of leading in such complex conditions yields an increase in pastoral turnover, leaving many congregations ill-equipped to pursue a vision of ministry. This progressive rate of pastoral turnover and lack of succession planning means that many new pastors frequently assume pastorates in unpredictable and unstable congregations. They encounter low morale in the congregation and confusion amongst lay leaders about the church's direction. Interestingly, new pastors often need the same skills required of turnaround CEOs who are charged with leading a declining company.

Previously, specialists who took over ailing organizations restored them to health with their distinct expertise, skills, and insights. Among them were pastors who restructured churches and made some radical, short-term decisions that maintained a congregation's viability. Whereas these brief fixes kept churches afloat, in essence they were only "Band-Aid" approaches that enabled the pastor who enjoyed an interim tenure to depart as a hero in the congregation's eyes. Today, helping a church "turn the corner" does not suffice for genuine pastoral leadership.

Transitional congregations need "GPS Pastors" who have versatile leadership skills, enabling them to adapt reasonably within constantly changing environments. A GPS Pastor strives for successful, sustainable change. Often, churches fail to realize the positive potential of change. These gaps between bold aspirations and formidable challenges undermine progress toward transition to new realities. Pastors have an obligation to consult available expertise and research as they respond to rapidly shifting trends in their churches and society. This adaptable leadership approach empowers pastors to improvise as they prudently experiment with innovative strategies. Pastors should always seek mutually beneficial relationships, more effective means of communication, and fluid interactions that help lay leaders and congregants apply and surpass the wisdom of today's experts.[25] GPS Pastors have learned to overcome the Moses mentality found in the 18th chapter of Exodus. In this text we find that Moses had his hands in all of the major and minor disputes of the Children of Israel. As a result, his father-in-law, Jethro, told him that he must learn to delegate the minor disputes and responsibilities to others and focus his time on the major disputes and decisions. GPS Pastors understand that leading is not doing the work of ten people but influencing ten people to work. Practically speaking, GPS Pastors find new maps to guide congregational transition.

The reason this is important for a congregation in transition is that adaptive leadership assembles courageous people who willingly and straightforwardly confront tough challenges to enable a church to thrive through transitions. GPS Pastors expect and embrace adversity and challenges by transforming competing interests into assets for

---

25 Ronald Heifetz, Alexander Grashow and Marty Linsky, The Practice of Adaptive Leadership: Tools and Tactics for Changing Your Organization and the World (Boston: Cambridge Leadership Associates, 2009) 2.

progress and success. GPS Pastors harness the power of vision; they cast a vision that inspires and motivates, as vision is the glue that holds everyone together in transition. GPS Pastors understand that a sober and balanced vision serves as the road map to success.

Additionally, GPS Pastors accept the prerequisite of internal changes before the realization of external goals. They, therefore, concentrate closely on how residual effects of personal transitions influence congregational change. To become GPS Pastors, pastors must grapple with their own personal fears and perceptions regarding transitions in their lives so they can become sensitive to the planning and implementation of transitional strategies for the congregations they serve. The way in which a pastor handles personal transitions foreshadows his or her leadership approach as it relates to congregational transitions. Relying on the unquestionable, constant nature of change, GPS Pastors utilize its inevitability to achieve progress in a church's ministry.

For GPS Pastors, factors are friends. Factors uncovered or revealed from conducting Strengths, Weaknesses, Opportunities and Threats (SWOT) analysis of the congregation can be hard to accept for both pastor and congregation. However, this information is necessary for vision casting and transitional strategies.

Thus, GPS Pastors...

1. ...are mission minded leaders who have a clear sense of what they have to do.
2. ...know how to leverage power. They use their influence to get the right people on board to participate in the transition.
3. ...spend time conducting research and examining the area that needs change. Nehemiah spent time examining the wall before he formed a strategy for rebuilding (Nehemiah 2:13).
4. ...adapt to adversity and challenges. While most people run from them, GPS Pastors expect them. Wherever change and progress are underway, competing interests inevitably rise to challenge them. At that point, pastors or leaders will have to

decide whether they will accept and meet the challenge or fall back into the opposition's agenda.

5. ...know that change is constant and that it permeates all transitions.

6. ...understand that they meet the congregation in the middle of the movie, and therefore must understand its history and DNA in order to effectively transition the ministry.

7. ...use the Bible as their key resource for transition. For example, Nehemiah's leadership skills moved the children of Israel through the challenging task of rebuilding the wall, and later rebuilding the people (Nehemiah 2-8).

8. ...delay preaching about vision for the first few months and concentrate their messages on addressing three factors: respect, trust, and listening. Before there is vision preaching there must be transition preaching. Transition preaching sets the stage for a stronger reception of the pastor's vision for the ministry.

9. ...understand that transition requires the collaboration of both pastor and congregation. Pastors should put together an advisory group (TMG) to assist with identifying transitional needs and address them through preaching. The advisory group should be a cross-section of the congregation. The group and pastor work together to gain a greater understanding of each other's struggles, fears, and convictions.

10. ...maintain a strong devotional life to insure personal integrity. Transitioning a ministry is very challenging, and just as with GPS Leaders, daily spiritual disciplines are essential to surviving the transition zone.

11. ...exercise patience in the transition zone. It took us six years to work through Oakdale's pastoral transition issues. We can put a timeline on change, but not on transition or the psychological impact of the change.

12. ...maintain balance at all times. Too much change will destroy the ministry while too little change will result in the ministry destroying itself. There must be a balance.

13. ...preach to the whole church. Preaching must speak to the various concerns of four generations: the Builders, Boomers, Busters, and Millennials. If you omit a group there will be problems in the ministry.

14. ...are humble enough to accept advice from others. By accepting the advice of his father-in-law, Jethro, Moses began overcoming the myth of indispensability. Jethro helped Moses come to grips with his need to delegate authority and responsibility to others in order to better meet the needs of the people (Ex. 18:13-26). A person who insists on "doing it all himself" may never get it all done. Perhaps merely a portion of it will get done, and that only marginally.

15. ...know that preaching is the most important activity for leading the congregation through a time of transition. Preaching unites, heals and brings Scripture alive. It also provides an opportunity to keep the church focused and centered. There will be members, trustees, deacons or representatives from a church council who believe that the focus must be on budgets or increased membership. While these are important for the life of the ministry, the pastor must use the preaching moment to remind people that their focus must be on Jesus Christ, who is constantly bringing change and shaping us into His image. Pastors who use preaching as a resource for moving through transitions both proclaim the Gospel of Jesus Christ and address the fears and concerns of their congregation. We help our congregations move from where they are toward a blessed future.

CHAPTER 9
APPLY DYNAMIC TRANSLATION
TO YOUR CONTEXT

Another important and creative tool that pastors and church leaders can use for understanding their congregation's movie and moving through their transition zone is dynamic translation. I was exposed to this resource while enrolled in the ACTS Doctorate of Ministry Program, and I found it be a creative way to demonstrate to the entire congregation the challenges of transition. Like a dramatic presentation, dynamic translation is a kind of role play that contemporizes a Bible story (so it speaks to our time) and contextualizes it (tuning into a specific moment and set of circumstances in life).[26] This dramatic technique had a favorable effect on helping Oakdale navigate the transition zone. Contextualizing the people and problems of the Bible allowed Oakdale congregants to step into the challenges of the biblical world as they faced their current situation of transition. The congregation and/or I became the main characters that thought, felt, spoke, and acted just as the biblical narrative suggested. Then we began applying these biblical truths to the Oakdale movie. For the first time, we created a powerful visual of the challenges and successes of biblical characters navigating their way through the transition zone of their time and demonstrating that transition will invoke an array of spiritual, physical, mental, and emotional reactions. Furthermore, these reactions are a normal part of transition.

Utilizing dynamic translation as a resource cannot be underestimated because in order for change to be navigated and fully embraced, it must

---

26 Charles H. Cosgrove and W. Dow Edgerton, *In Other Words: Incarnational Translation for Preaching* (Grand Rapids, MI: Eerdmans, 2007) 2.

be woven into the fabric of the congregation's spiritual development and formation structures. What better way to do this than to use the greatest book about change, the Bible, to show life in its creative ways?

Powerfully, Oakdale collectively stepped into the text and lived amongst the New Testament churches. As they grasped the challenges of first-century Christians in Corinth, Ephesus, Philippi, and throughout the vast Roman Empire, Oakdale congregants applied biblical answers and wisdom to their Chicago situations. The congregation and I fully embraced this process. We sat in the pews in Corinth and listened to Paul's strong letters. We cried with the Philippians as we heard of Paul's great love for our church. We feared for our lives with Paul and Luke during the great shipwreck at the end of Acts, and we lamented the divisions and separation in the Johannine community as 1 John records. We saw the biblical landscapes; smelled the pungent odors of livestock, human sweat, and sweltering heat; tasted Ancient Near Eastern cuisine; felt the heavy dust of unpaved roads, and touched the sunburned skin of fellow pilgrims to Jerusalem. As a consequence, sermons and Bible Study unfolded with incredible suspense as the congregation remained captivated from start to finish!

Additionally, dynamic translation is a creative way to increase attendance at weekly Bible study. Congregants were elated about participating as characters and set designers. Furthermore, many found that exploring the biblical world does not have to be dry and boring, but can be fun and exciting. This new approach breaks the monotony of parrot-like recitation of a passage or didactic instruction. Attendees benefit tremendously as their minds and hearts are opened to new understandings of the Bible, its people, and its cultural setting.

An unfulfilled ministry goal of Pastor Jemison in the final years of his pastoral tenure is a powerful example of how Dynamic Biblical Translation can be used to bring clarity to God's will for a transitioning congregation. The Pastor Emeritus desired to build a family life center for the community we serve. The grand opening of the facility was to coincide with his retirement celebration. However, community opposition along with other obstacles prevented completion of the center. Notwithstanding their overall support of the vision, members divided deeply about the timing of construction and fundraising, considering the forthcoming pastoral retirement and search for a successor. I arrived in the middle of this dramatic controversy, and it continued for another year and a half.

This Chicago dilemma at the dawn of the 21st century reminds me of King David's grave personal disappointment that he was unable to build the temple. As God's mysterious grace and providential design unfolds in David's life, his son, Solomon, assumes his father's heartfelt dream. Practically, David prepares the foundation for the temple construction by storing wood, gold, and other materials. As He allows David to contribute to building the temple, God does not forsake David or nullify his dream. Yet God specifically designates Solomon for the task. As it relates to Oakdale's family life center, the Pastor Emeritus was able to cast the vision in an effective way and timely manner, but I received the sanction to complete the actual building of the center. With the assistance of the TMG, I translated David's dilemma into the Oakdale context of my predecessor's personal disappointment but eventual victory in the completion of the project.[27]

As his successor, I assured the Pastor Emeritus of my support for his vision, and I reserved the right to modify and expand the facility to meet future ministry needs. Regrettably, however, he misinterpreted my statements as a lack of support. More unfortunately, he and a small vocal minority extrapolated a wholesale negative characterization of his pastoral tenure at Oakdale from my remarks.

In response, the TMG recommended a dynamic translation based specifically upon 1 Chronicles 28:1-11 entitled, "When God Says No." The text reveals that David desired to build a temple to house the Ark of the Covenant, but despite David's righteous attitude, God says, "No, you are not to build a house for my Name" and then God specifically designates the task to Solomon. When God says no to our

---

27 Please see 1 Chronicles 28 and 29 to read the complete story of David's aspirations to build the temple.

personal ambitions and preferences, we respond affirmatively to His will. Furthermore, we concretize our obedience in verbal, physical, and financial support. Ultimately, David saves the necessary money and stores materials that Solomon uses to build the temple. My dynamic translation of this passage illuminated Oakdale's struggles of balancing the unfinished vision of a revered former pastor and the new direction of his successor.

The TMG made the foregoing passage relevant. In its adaptation, the Pastor Emeritus summoned the leaders of Oakdale: "I had it in my heart to build a family life center. I commissioned an architect to design the center as the Lord revealed His will. I secured the funding. I planned its completion before my retirement. But God said, 'You are not to build a family life center.' He chose my successor to fulfill this vision."

Additionally, we developed an equally effective sermon on the family life center. We shared our understanding of God's will relating to this ongoing dilemma. Not surprisingly, the congregation responded with different levels of enthusiasm to such an intense sermonic occasion. Some parishioners described this sermon as a therapy session. Others felt a blessed assurance that God is in control. Still others recognized futility in arguing with God's Word. The method of dynamic translation coupled with congregational feedback equipped me to implement very sensitive changes without backlash. It is an approach I highly recommend for any church.

Again, I cannot emphasize enough the important role that dynamic translation can play in navigating a transition. It becomes another opportunity to understand the congregation's movie and to drill home the new direction of the ministry. Many of the congregants will not fully comprehend the new direction through only the Sunday morning experiences. Pastors and church leaders must understand that full conversion of the congregation to the new direction of the ministry will most likely occur as a result of weaving the necessary components of change into Bible Study classes, Sunday school curriculum, and small group material.

CHAPTER 10

PASTOR, TAKE CARE OF YOURSELF SPIRITUALLY
DEVELOPING A SELF-CARE AGREEMENT

Once as I sat on an airplane preparing to dose off, I heard a flight attendant giving safety instructions. Although I had listened to these instructions many times in the past, I particularly heard the directive about the use of the overhead mask on this trip. She said, "In the unlikely event of a drop in cabin pressure, the overhead mask will drop. If you are sitting next to someone who is in need of assistance, please make sure you put your mask on before assisting the other person." If a caregiver preoccupies himself with assisting others and ignores his own needs, he puts everyone at risk. Transitional pastors and lay leaders must guard against neglecting spiritual self-care while they busily care for others.

A pastor's main resource for ministry is his or her spiritual and emotional wellbeing. Thus, how pastors attend to their own spiritual, physical, and emotional needs is crucial to their ability to serve and navigate the transition zone. When the pastor is in poor shape spiritually, physically, or emotionally, the ministry is compromised and the pastor frustrated. Although pastors are ultimately responsible for their own spiritual health and wellbeing, the congregation must make every effort to ensure that the pastor is equipped with resources to maintain spiritual vitality. Self-care was something that came to the forefront while navigating the complex Oakdale transition.

In my sixth year of ministry at Oakdale, I learned of the necessity of spiritual direction and more fully understood the need for self-care. I recall feeling rather overwhelmed by the strain of our congregation's constant changes and transitions. I felt as though I were spiraling downward spiritually. Navigating our transition had taken a considerable physical, spiritual, and emotional toll; my spiritual life was a mess. I was reading the Bible only for sermon preparation and thus I was not spending enough time reflecting on Scripture for personal spiritual enrichment. Books on transition and change had replaced the Scriptures as my devotional reading. My quiet time with God became non-existent. It became filled with additional board meetings, hospital visits, calls, and many days and nights of transitional strategy meetings.

I exhausted myself emotionally by busily brokering compromises between the many fractional and opinionated groups at Oakdale – all with the objective of achieving a stronger church. I failed to count the cost to my emotional wellbeing. "Cranky and on edge about everything" described me. Simply put, I was not a pleasant person to be around. Not realizing the problem was internal. I reasoned everyone else had a problem. Although I love the feeling of exhilaration after completing a challenging workout, I somehow stopped weight and endurance training. Regrettably, I felt I was just too busy to fit that into my schedule. I convinced myself that my time was better spent directing our transition efforts. Consequently, I gained a significant amount of weight, which led to additional health challenges. One Sunday after morning worship, my physician, who is a member of our congregation, pulled me aside to share his concerns about my weight gain and long hours. He warned me that poor physical health would lead to a serious crash that would adversely affect me, my family, and the church.

I convinced myself that I only had this moment "to strike the hot iron" of our transition experience or I would lose forever these key moments. I planned to take time off and relax once Oakdale had navigated a few additional and significant transitional hurdles — then I would regain my balance in life. I did not fully comprehend the reality that transition is a work that remains in progress. In fact, transitional work never ends. There is always something that is changing in the congregation, and these changes continue to move pastors and church leaders toward a new set of transitional challenges.

In *The Pastor as Spiritual Guide*, Howard Rice accentuates the dangers of a pastoral vocation. He states, "Sometimes the profession of ministry has not strengthened the faith of those called to this vocation. The pastoral vocation has caused them to become immune to the very Gospel they have proclaimed. Words such as "Gospel," "forgiveness," and "new life" may seem to apply only to parishioners and not to pastors themselves."[28] I contend that pastors in transition significantly increase their vocational hazards because of the complexity of transitional decisions and rapidity of change. Rice further states, "Many pastors have no one to whom they can turn for advice, correction, or encouragement. They do not dare speak of their most intimate needs and desires with those within the congregation for fear of destroying the pastoral relationship."[29] This is particularly important for pastors and leaders in the transition zone to understand. Pastors have a tendency to get so consumed with the work of navigating their congregations that they forget to care for themselves.

In response to a mentor's advice relating to my need for spiritual guidance and self-care, I discovered spiritual direction, which enabled my survival during Oakdale's transitional period and helped me regain intimacy in my relationship with Christ. In short, spiritual direction reignited the fire of my pastoral calling. Facilitators introduced me to centuries-old spiritual traditions and practices helpful in discerning God's will and persevering on a genuine spiritual journey. More practically, silent retreats, spiritual readings, and one-on-one meetings with a spiritual director encouraged me in developing an even deeper relationship with Christ. I would argue that every pastor, regardless of location in the transition zone, should consider spiritual direction.

Spiritual direction originates within Catholic tradition, which scholars trace to the fourth century desert fathers. Many Protestants, particularly disciples in conservative congregations such as Oakdale, react to spiritual direction with ambivalence and distrust. Yet spiritual

---

28 Howard Rice, *The Pastor as Spiritual Guide* (Nashville: Upper Room Books, 1998) 156.
29 Rice, 161.

direction is quickly permeating Christendom as an effective method to deepen one's relationship with God. Mainline Protestant denominations are adapting this spiritual practice to fit the ethos of their theological traditions. For example, the Evangelical Covenant Churches of America, with which Oakdale is formally affiliated, established the North Park Center for Spiritual Direction.[30]

In its simplest form, spiritual direction utilizes listening, discernment, and prayer in a confidential setting of encouragement and compassion. A spiritual companion listens to another person's life stories to help him or her discern God's presence and work of the Holy Spirit. In *Sacred Companions: The Gift of Spiritual Friendship and Direction*, David G. Benner offers a very insightful definition of spiritual direction: "a prayer process in which a person seeking help in cultivating a deeper personal relationship with God meets with another for prayer and conversation that is focused on increasing awareness of God in the midst of life experiences and facilitating surrender to God's will."[31]

Pastors and congregants generally seek a spiritual director because they need to be heard by someone whom they trust as they articulate their deepest spiritual questions and concerns. For many, life's daily busyness eclipses God's presence and providential actions. Pastors and church leaders increasingly find it difficult to notice God's mystery and magnificence. Clergy who primarily provide counseling and guidance for congregants realize that their ever-increasing responsibilities leave little time for one-on-one spiritual direction. A spiritual director serves as a companion and tour guide on the spiritual journey, pointing out God's presence and actions. He or she listens attentively, without pressuring the other person to agree with his or her perspective. The spiritual director does not coerce the directee to share anything he or she is not ready to express.

The term "director" is strong and slightly misleading because it suggests one person telling another person what to believe and how to

30 I earned a Certificate in Spiritual Direction in August 2009.
31 David G. Benner, *Sacred Companions: The Gift of Spiritual Friendship and Direction* (Downers Grove: InterVarsity Press, 2002) 94.

act. Actually, a spiritual director encourages and empowers other people instead of managing their lives for them. As the term "companion" is less formal and authoritarian, it possibly would not be as widely accepted in our world of titles and prestige. Other appropriate terms include "spiritual guide" and "soul friend."

Spiritual direction is not counseling or psychotherapy. As a pastor who frequently counsels, I had to understand this significant distinction. Spiritual direction utilizes a person's primary and genuine desire to mature as a spiritual being along with reason, Scripture, the practice of spiritual disciplines, religious tradition, and experience to accomplish this objective. In contrast, pastoral counseling, analytical psychology, and various types of psychotherapy address the problems of a person's psyche, problems usually originating in childhood experiences.

Nurturing a relationship with Almighty God is the principal means of spiritual direction in redressing daily, practical, and personal challenges. The mottos of two churches in New York City capture this purpose: (1) "Giving people faith and power to face life's difficulties with Christian maturity" and (2) "We are the Community's Church – Encouraging and Empowering People with Faith to Embrace Life with Christ's Power." Persons who suffer with more complex emotional problems and longstanding psychological and intrapersonal dilemmas will need the assistance of a trained psychotherapist or psychiatrist. It is imperative that pastors and leaders understand this reality. Because of the difficulty of my transition zone, I was under the care of both a spiritual director and a therapist. The therapist provided the resources to assist me psychologically, and my spiritual director provided me with resources to see how God was operating in my life and ministry.

Howard Rice argues that regular practice of spiritual disciplines protects individuals from exhausting themselves and depleting their spiritual resources. Especially for pastors, these practices guard against spiritual burnout. Pastors exhibit this emptiness when they operate on fumes by going through the motions of ministry without passion. Regular attention to the care of one's own soul is not optional for pastors. Spiritual self-care during a transition zone may be the only means to serve effectively and continually without losing one's soul. Accordingly, each pastor needs a wise guide who will warn him as he approaches dangerous cliffs. The climb for success and excellence in pastoral ministry is too challenging to attempt alone.

I vividly recall my first spiritual direction session in which my director introduced me to *Lectio Divina*. This ancient Christian practice yields a "divine reading" by listening attentively and prayerfully to Scripture. The method offers four dimensions of a biblical passage: *Lectio* — reading God's Word to ascertain what Christ, the Personified Word of God, is conveying; *Meditatio* — reflecting on God's Word to hear how Christ speaks to me; *Oratio* — responding to God's Word to understand what Christ invites me to do; and *Contemplatio* — resting in the presence of God's Word. We read and listened to a few isolated verses of Scripture without analyzing them. We sat in silence before God, listening for revelation from the passage. We repeated this process. *Lectio Divina* offered a fresh method of listening and connecting to God's Word.

Additionally, my spiritual director asked me to create a Rule of Life (the focus of Chapter 11). This checklist of intentional spiritual practices and personal habits maintains and deepens one's relationship with God. Living with a Rule of Life assures accountability of spiritual practice. As it forces me to examine all aspects of my professional and personal life, living by a Rule of Life is one of the most difficult assignments I have ever undertaken. My initial self-diagnosis revealed a number of blind spots in my spiritual life. As a result, I began to focus more clearly on the spiritual, physical, emotional, and vocational activities in my daily routines.

To address these deficiencies and position myself for the rigors of the transition zone, I redesigned my daily schedule to develop consistent holy habits of prayer, silence, fasting, and journaling. These spiritual habits are important because they enable pastors and church leaders to persevere whether they are in a time of testing or season of success. We practice daily hygiene of brushing our teeth, combing our hair, and taking a shower regardless of our mood. We practice holy habits as a spiritual hygiene without conscious thought until they become equally ingrained within us.

For pastors and church leaders in transition, silent retreats are one of the most impactful spiritual practices. At first, I was uncomfortable going to a retreat center with only my Bible and journal and sitting in complete silence for two days. Living in the city of Chicago and being an avid consumer of myriad stimuli of modern technology, I thought it rather strange that I would hear from God in total silence because I preferred a facilitator with spiritual exercises. However, a silent retreat became the path that led me back to an intimate relationship with God. It really helped me become more responsive to God's presence in my daily life. The competing demands of marriage, fatherhood of two very young children, and pastoral ministry often left little time for daily spiritual reflection. Not surprisingly, I sometimes missed God's actions in my daily life or faith community. My family and work routine, admittedly noble in purpose and practice, were preventing me from being with God. Sacred solitude ushered me into the presence of God unlike I had ever experienced it before. The silent retreats remove the noise of ministry long enough for God to speak in fresh ways of the new direction and ministry toward which He's calling the congregation.

Spiritual direction continues to anchor me while navigating the transition zone. I am stronger and healthier physically, mentally, and spiritually, and now I create boundaries around my personal life. While I can choose to do anything, I realize I cannot do everything. Therefore, I select a few projects and shepherd them through the maze of transition. Spiritual direction has strengthened the quality of my marriage and family time. I understand the importance of maintaining a regular Sabbath. "What keeps the fire burning in the fire place? Space between the logs. If you want to keep burning you need space from your hectic life."[32] Pastors must remember the necessity of creating space between their ministry responsibilities so they can keep burning for Christ.

---

32 Fire by Judy Brown. June 8, 2010, March 28, 2012. <http://soulcare.com/_blog/Mindy's_Blog/post/Fire_and_Breathing_Space>

Additionally, spiritual direction yielded such rejuvenation in my ministry that I incorporated its best practices in Oakdale's Christian formation system. We now utilize silent retreats, *Lectio Divina*, discernment, Sabbath, and meetings with a spiritual director; the spiritual dividends are immeasurable. I have a pastor's indescribable joy watching spiritual direction positively influence our transition.

Further, integrating the language and concepts of spiritual direction into my congregational context led to spiritual renewal and healing for Oakdale and me. We are revisiting traditions with a greater appreciation of our heritage. This journey to "home" allows us to touch the core of our souls. Spiritual direction provides missing pieces to the puzzle of our experiences and being. Joyously, we have begun the journey and are moving toward a more fulfilling life in Christ and fellowship with one another.

Acquiring a Ministry Coach and Mentor

Each day in the transition zone, I looked for support and guidance. As the senior pastor and along with the lay leadership, I made critical choices about the future direction of Oakdale. We had to consider how these difficult decisions would affect the congregation and the community in decades ahead. We consulted helpful resources from conferences and workshops on change and church growth, and we spent a lot of time contextualizing the information to meet our needs. Still, there were a number of unanswered questions.

As we sought someone with requisite time and skills to walk alongside us, a TMG member suggested I explore coaching and mentoring programs that provide weekly or bi-weekly one-on-one conversations offering strategies for transition and growth since I personally needed time when my concerns were the focal point.[33] As with many other pastoral colleagues, I "tend to forget that remaining centered ourselves and anchored in God are acts of faithfulness,

---

33 Craig A. Satterlee, *When God Speaks Through Change: Preaching In Times of Congregational Transition* (Vital Worship, Healthy Congregations) (Herndon: The Alban Institute, 2005) 107.

strength, and mature leadership. We seek balance, refreshment, health, and wholeness so that we can better serve the people and ministry to which God calls us."[34]

The idea of a coach for pastors greatly intrigued me. Where does one find a ministry coach? Armed with this suggestion, I began researching the possibilities and discovered *Christian Coaching: Helping Others Turn Potential into Reality* by Gary Collins. He defines coaching as "the art and practice of guiding a person or group from where they are toward the greater competence and fulfillment that they desire."[35] Christian coaching empowers pastors to progress from vocational stalemate to a divinely ordained and orchestrated existential space. Coaching expands vision, builds confidence, unlocks potential, hones skills, and provides practical steps to reach goals. Considering contemporary demands for numerical congregational growth, coaching is one of the most effective tools for pastors and church leaders in clarifying purpose and goals as they change and grow.

Churches reluctantly use coaching to equip various ministries. In 2001, Gary Collins expressed concern that virtually no churches were utilizing the principles and techniques of coaching even though it was the "hottest" new profession in America.[36]

While coaching for pastors is relatively new in the ecclesiastical realm, its benefits are very well known in most other professions. Athletics, music, acting, and fitness coaches are often the determining factor in achieving success and training their clients for greater effectiveness. Without good coaches, most celebrities in entertainment, fine and performing arts, and professional athletics would not reach the pinnacle of their performance and success.

In business and industry, rapid marketplace shifts impact daily decision-making. Effective leaders cultivate versatility to improve skills and to develop new abilities to meet the constant and changing

---

34 Satterlee, 97.
35 Gary R. Collins, Ph.D., *Christian Coaching: Helping Others Turn Potential Into Reality* (Colorado Springs: Navpress, 2001) 15.
36 Collins, 15.

demands of market fluctuations. The church is not exempt from these dramatic and unpredictable economic, sociological, and demographic trends. Therefore, pastors benefit greatly from seeing coaching and mentoring programs as a necessity rather than a luxury.

A coach is not an instructor, counselor, or consultant. He or she supports ministers and lay leaders as they bear the burdens and reap the blessings of transitioning a congregation toward a new vision of ministry. Coaching provides accountability in decision making. It also expands the skills and abilities of leaders to foster new direction in their context.

As I searched for coaching programs, I was unaware that my denomination, the Evangelical Covenant Church of America, officially recognizes coaching as a valuable opportunity for pastors and ministry leaders who struggle in transition and growth. Denominational leaders established a formal relationship with Ministry Advantage (www. ministryadvantage.org), a coaching company based in Dallas, Texas that specializes in weekly one-on-one and "in-the-trenches training" for pastors.

The personnel of Ministry Advantage made significant strides in coaching and mentoring before "coaching" became a trendy concept in professional literature and circles. Their passion for preparing leaders for success evolved into a comprehensive systems approach that enhances leadership capabilities for individuals and organizations across a wide spectrum. Succinctly, they create clarity, reduce conflict, and persuade a congregation to accept new direction.

Coaching imparted the tools with which we turned our vision into reality. It resembled receiving the right prescription for your eyeglasses; the fuzziness disappeared and our way became clear. My coach pushed me toward tasks I preferred to avoid in order to become the pastor and person I always desired to be.

It was refreshing and encouraging to talk with someone who said 'I did that once,' or 'We tried that last year,' or 'You probably don't want to do that.' With my coach's consultation, Oakdale and I developed a transitional strategic plan that included discarding ineffective approaches and adjusting to changes in "real time" to maximize results.

Another support ministry that contributed to the success of our transition was Ministry Mentors (website www.ministrymentors.org). A spiritually based organization offering supportive professional relationships, Ministry Mentors focuses primarily on a pastor's needs. They also design clergy collegial groups of five persons who meet weekly or even monthly. These clusters consist of pastors from various denominations, ages, and ethnicity. Meetings include intercessory praying for each member as well as book discussions and exchanging ideas about best ministry practices. It is liberating to share confidentially with fellow pastors about daily ministry struggles and personal family challenges.

In many ways, Paul's letters to the churches are the words of a coach and mentor seeking to strengthen, encourage, and enlighten first century and contemporary disciples in becoming more effective ambassadors for Christ. In addition to their private prayer, meditation and devotion, pastors and lay leaders practically discern the will of God through collaborative relationships with coaches and peers. These invaluable and individual resources will guide an anxious congregation through its similar transition.

CHAPTER 11

ADOPT AND FOLLOW A RULE OF LIFE

One of the tools to help pastors and church leaders protect themselves against burnout and maintain a vibrant spiritual life in the transition zone is adopting and following a Rule of Life. In the midst of a busy ministry life, many pastors find it difficult to notice God's actions in their daily lives, and the truth is that for many pastors and parishioners alike, the resources that can help give such spiritual clarity have been profoundly limited.

I saw a quote on a billboard that said, "The beginning of anything of significance is a plan." As I began the journey of deepening my relationship with Christ, I discovered the need for a better plan. I desperately needed a strong spiritual contract, a "Rule of Life." I needed attainable goals and an intentional pattern to foster spiritual growth each day. Living by a Rule of Life remains one of the most difficult assignments I have ever undertaken because it forces me to examine all aspects of my life: spiritual, physical, emotional, and vocational. Furthermore, I painstakingly confront poor habits as I redirect my priorities toward personal development and spiritual growth.

For example, in 2004, I started a self-care program, "Faith, Family and Fitness." I intended this self-care program as a time to build up my faith through prayer, Bible study, and reflection. I also planned to spend quality time with my family while maintaining a weekly fitness routine. Unsurprisingly and without explanation or excuse, I admit this self-care program fell off of my list of priorities. I imprisoned myself within the maze of parish ministry because ministry does not lend itself to a well-written, three-page job description with definable duties, limitations of time, and enumerated responsibilities. The endless nature of pastoral ministry never ceases to amaze me. There is always someone or something requiring my attention, whether I am visiting a congregant in the hospital, attending meetings, or preparing a sermon, and these demands leave very little time for self-care. Nonetheless, I realize that adhering to a Rule of Life encourages and empowers me to maintain healthy boundaries.

Thus, adopting and following a Rule of Life has emerged as a much-needed resource that can be embraced and utilized by pastors and parishioners as a means for maintaining a healthy spiritual life and ministry. According to Robert A Gallagher, author of *A Rule of Life*, a Rule of Life is the means by which an individual Christian establishes an intentional pattern of Christian discipline which can, over time, be reflected upon, revised, and deepened. A Rule of Life is an expression of the faith and practice of the whole church in one's own life, a discipline freely taken on to give order, support, and direction to one's life, and a means of rooting one's life in Christ. As each of our lives is unique, so each rule will have a somewhat different shape.

Further, a Rule of Life is an intentional pattern of spiritual disciplines that provides structure and direction for growth in holiness and establishes a rhythm for life that is helpful in being formed by the Spirit, a rhythm that reflects a love for God and respect for how He has made us. As such, The Rule of Life should include three things: a self-assessment, an explanation of how you will practice your chosen disciplines, and your form of accountability. First, provide a clear self-assessment that briefly describes your current situation in life-family responsibilities, work schedule, and other life circumstances. Your self-assessment should also reflect on the strengths and weaknesses of your character. Second, describe the way in which you will practice specific disciplines. Your Rule of Life should include an explanation of why your choices not only fit your situation in life but also how they address areas where you especially need discipline and growth.

Finally, once you have chosen your spiritual disciplines and explained your choices, state who will hold you accountable and pray for you as you practice your Rule of life. For this role, consider a friend, a small group, or a spiritual director.

The Rule of Life, very simply, is an intentional, conscious plan to keep God at the center of everything we do. It provides guidelines to help us intentionally pay attention and remember Him. The meaning of Rule comes from the Greek word for "trellis," a tool designed to enable a grapevine to get off the ground and grow upward, becoming more fruitful and productive. In the same way, a Rule of Life can be the trellis that helps us abide in Christ and become more fruitful spiritually. If you don't set your own priorities others will set priorities for you; nowhere is this truer than with your spiritual life. To make this clearer, below are excerpts of my personal Rule of Life.

Spiritually

"Wherefore I put thee in remembrance that thou stir up the gift of God, which is in thee by the putting on of my hands. For God hath not given us the spirit of fear; but of power, and of love, and of a sound mind." (2 Timothy 1:6-7)

The length of my devotional time began to shrink to the point of meaninglessness. This reality was disheartening as I have always enjoyed a strong and vibrant devotional life during most of my adult years. There was a time when I spent an hour or two praying, studying, and reflecting on a daily basis. These spiritual disciplines are the foundation of my relationship with Christ. However, with marriage and the addition of children, I began to struggle for periods of withdrawal and spiritual empowerment. Today, regrettably, most of my prayer, study, and reflection centers upon sermon preparation and teaching responsibilities. Extended neglect of personal practice of spiritual disciplines adversely affects my insight and effectiveness.

Several months ago, a member of my congregation asked me a question that led to soul searching for nearly two weeks. Simple and innocent, her question was quite profound. I did not expect the feelings that surfaced. "Pastor, do you still dream like you did when you first arrived at Oakdale"? I asked, "Why would you ask this question?" Over the course of the last year, she observed I sometimes seemed downcast and disconnected. Perhaps my neophyte fever had broken and the passions of our new relationship as Pastor and people were cooling. Furthermore, she noted that I was a definite dreamer upon my arrival at Oakdale. My dreams inspired her and people within her circle of friends. She admired the way I looked beyond the obstacles of our transition toward the divine and providential opportunities. My preaching relayed my optimism for Oakdale's future.

Although the question emotionally startled me, I initially responded, "Yes, I am still a dreamer." However, when other congregants also asked this question, I began to cry as I was unaware of the pressure our transition was having upon me. Everyone saw it except me. It greatly saddened me to realize I had stopped growing spiritually.

Today, I ensure I continue growing spiritually. I have a standing daily appointment with God. During this special meeting, I spend ten minutes reading a daily devotional, twenty minutes studying a particular chapter of the Bible, fifteen minutes writing in my journal, and fifteen minutes praying. I commit this hour to character development and spiritual empowerment in addition to my sermon preparation and Bible study time.

I also include fasting twice a week as a part of my spiritual growth. During Lent from Ash Wednesday to Good Friday, I fast for 40 days, abstaining from certain foods and drinks. I base this fast on the dietary restrictions in the book of Daniel. By far the most difficult spiritual discipline I practice, fasting requires a steadfast determination, yet it is one of the most helpful means of deepening my relationship with Jesus.

Physically

"Don't you know that your body is the temple of the Holy Spirit, who lives in you and was given to you by God? You do not belong to yourself, for God brought you with a high price. So you must honor God with your body." 1 Corinthians 6:19-20 (NLT)

Throughout my ministry, I diligently cared for my body through good diet and exercise. At one point, I was a vegetarian for nearly four years. Also, I participated in semi-pro physical exercise competitions. Despite the exhilaration and practical rewards of intensive physical activity, I have allowed the competing demands of family, ministry, and other distractions to pull me away from a regular workout regimen.

Now, I commit to physical exercise four times weekly from 7:00 a.m. to 8:30 a.m. I connect with two friends as accountability partners. Combined with regular physicals and visits to my doctor, exercise equips me to maintain a healthy lifestyle.

Vocationally

"Study to shew thyself approved unto God, a workman that needeth not be ashamed, rightly dividing the word of truth." (2 Timothy 2:15, KJV)

I have always been committed to continuing professional education and cutting edge vocational development. Once, my predecessor made a profound statement. He correlated his personal, spiritual, and vocational growth with that of the congregation. Pastor Jemison challenged me to grow continually through workshops, classes, books, and networking. Subsequently, I pursued and earned a Doctor of Ministry degree. I established a reading regimen of two books a quarter relating to preaching, teaching, and leading. I also participate in three vision tours a year.

Emotionally

"Make every effort to add to your faith goodness; and to goodness, knowledge; and to knowledge, self-control; and to self-control, perseverance; and to perseverance, godliness; and to godliness, brotherly kindness; and to brotherly kindness, love." (2 Peter 1:5-7) "For if you possess these qualities in increasing measure, they will keep you from being ineffective and unproductive in your knowledge of our Lord Jesus Christ."(2 Peter 1:8)

I try very hard to incorporate the meaning of those two Scriptures into my life so my emotional well-being and relationship with Christ will be effective personally and professionally. In the past, I did not always have clear boundaries to cultivate my growth spiritually, physically, and mentally. I spent almost ten years trying to convince myself that my ministry was also my hobby. Between meetings, counseling, travel, and administration details, I rarely took a day off. In fact, I hardly cared for myself. After pastoral ministry and family, self-care always came last.

"Husbands, love your wives, even as Christ also loved the church, and gave himself for it." (Ephesians 5:25) This verse exhorts me to understand the old adage that ministry begins at home and spreads abroad. I cannot love the church at the expense of my priestly duties to my family. I must love my family as Christ loves the Church. In essence, I put my family first. A venerable clergy colleague advises, "If you are going to short change anyone or anything, let it be the church because God calls you to love your family first and foremost."

Monday is my personal Sabbath. I have a work-free zone in my house. There are signs through the house and particularly in my home office that read, "Your home is a work-free zone. You do not work in the family zone; spend time with your family. Your first ministry is to you and your family." Another sign says, "Sermons must be done by Thursday. A sermon is work; therefore it must be prepared at work but never in the family zone." On Mondays, I re-energize and reconnect. During Friday evenings and Saturday mornings, my family has my undivided attention.

However difficult it is to adhere faithfully to The Rule of Life, it establishes necessary boundaries for comprehensive and continual development spiritually, physically, emotionally, and vocationally.

CHAPTER 12
IF NECESSARY, CHANGE YOUR WORSHIP STYLE

As one of the means of wading through the muddy waters of transition, I hosted several workshops focusing on transitional concerns. We spent four weeks reading and discussing *Who Moved My Church?*[37] and our conversations uncovered a tremendous anxiety. However, our collective study produced a pivotal moment as I addressed a "Third Rail" issue: Oakdale's Sunday morning worship service and, primarily, the music.

Oakdale's Sunday morning worship service was the centerpiece of the ministry. In fact, for the majority of members, the Sunday morning worship was the only ministry activity they attended and were willing to participate in. In our context as a predominately African American congregation, music plays a key role in worship. As a young pastor, I remember asking The Reverend Anthony Trufant, senior pastor of Emmanuel Baptist Church of Brooklyn, how he revitalized an aging congregation from a few hundred people to well over 4,000 in attendance on Sunday. He told me that one of the major contributing factors to their growth was music. He shared with me: "Dee, you must never underestimate the power of music to transform lives. It is a universal language. It has the power to unite and divide. However, for many people the worship music can touch in ways that the preaching moment cannot. In fact, many people attend worship more for the music than the preaching. Therefore, you must pay close attention to how the music is impacting the congregation." I know many congregations who can trace

---

37 Mike Nappa, *Who Moved My Church? A Story About Discovering Purpose in a Changing Culture* (Tulas: River Oak Publishing, 2001).

their significant growth or decline directly to how they handle the music component of their worship service.

Even though worship was the most important event at Oakdale, the worship music was no longer meeting the needs of individuals. The congregation desperately needed to retain or attract new people groups such as young families, young adults, and youth. Oakdale faced the same challenge that most mainline congregations face—an aging congregation with declining attendance. Oakdale's worship style appealed mostly to those who were attracted to a very traditional worship music style, and it completely alienated others. Our music mix of hymns, anthems, and traditional gospel created an atmosphere of formality and constraint.

Although it was quite obvious the first day I assumed the leadership of Oakdale that the worship music needed to change, I could sense that any discussion of changing our worship format would incite a deadly riot that would leave much casualty in its wake. I have seen many churches destroyed over controversies surrounding worship style, and I did not want Oakdale to be one of them. Therefore, if I was going to tamper with the worship service, and particularly the music, I needed to proceed with extreme caution. At Oakdale, it seemed like everyone had an opinion about what type of worship music was needed or not needed in order to create the perfect worship experience. Every week, I found myself in conversations with a number of visitors, particularly young adults, regarding Oakdale's worship music. I would often hear comments such as, "Pastor, when are you going to address the worship music? It is really painful to hear." Another person commented, "Pastor, the music was a complete disconnect. You really need to do something about the music."

Thus, within the first six to eight months, the issue of worship music was on my transitional radar with full force. The ministry was grinding to a standstill because of our worship music. In every one of my TMG meetings, the worship music was the center of our discussion. Some were saying that we needed to change our worship music immediately;

others insisted the music was fine. I was sensitive to everyone's comments on both sides. Since I could see the pain that any change would inflict, I was reluctant to address the issue head on. However, two individuals from our TMG pulled me aside to inform me that our worship music issues were moving from simmering to bubbling up into a full worship war. They told me that it was my responsibly as the pastor to step forward and lead the congregation through any change of worship music or style. I remember going back to my office that day, closing the door, and getting down on my knees to ask God for a plan to address our worship music without destroying the congregation. In fact, I went on a 21-day fast to seek God's guidance around our transitional issues and particularly our worship.

God led me to contact several pastors and worship leaders who offered advice and provided a number of worship resources. The first thing I discovered was the importance of my role as a worship leader. In fact, the pastor is the chief worship leader of any congregation. In many cases the congregation will follow the worship tone set by the pastor and the leadership. Therefore, I had to understand true worship and the role of music in worship. Worship comes from an old English word "worth-shape." In other words, whatever we worship shapes us. For example, l learned that worship has the potential to bring people before God, and it opens people up to God. The Bible records in John 4:20-24, "God is seeking true worshippers."

My worship research reminded us to be careful not to change our worship style or format just for the sake of change or to try force people into accepting the latest worship craze. We formed a commission on worship, which comprised a cross-section of the congregation ranging in age from 15 to 80. This group of twelve men, women, and youth examined our worship services for about eight weeks with the primary goal of identifying resources and solutions for navigating through our worship war.

After eight weeks of researching, surveying, and listening to the congregation regarding worship, we had a town hall meeting to discuss the findings. The worship commission was able to articulate much better than I that our worship style must change or the congregation would die; I did not have the tenure to say it as bluntly as they could. The commission firmly stated that our very survival as a congregation depended on changing our worship style and particularly our music. They shared that some congregants would likely leave because they would not accept this change of worship format. The decision to leave would be unfortunate and cause a great deal of sadness for the congregation, but it was unavoidable. We cannot be held hostage by a format or preference that could threaten our future. The commission emphasized that rather than changing minds, polarizing debates would create a deeper wedge in our congregation. They pointed out the importance of having a written worship plan to help us understand what a successful worship experience would look like and what types of music would enhance our worship. Another aspect of the commission's report reminded the congregation that spiritual maturity would be required in order to worship in different ways, especially when it was outside of our comfort zone.

The major turning point of our worship wars was when I decided to use testimonies to illustrate our worship music challenges. Hearing one another talk about the disconnect between our praxis and our intent was powerful because it allowed everyone to see that whatever their position, they were not alone. At one of our *Who Moved My Church?* discussions, we successfully illustrated the challenges of worship so they were clear for everyone to see. Relying on Gary L. McIntosh's wisdom in *One Church, Four Generations: Understanding and Reaching All Ages in Your Church* and research from George Barna, I divided the congregation into four generational groups. The Builders (senior citizens) represented the views of persons born before 1945. "Baby Boomers" included persons born between 1946 and 1964. The "Busters," also known as "Generation X," were born between 1965 and 1983. Sociologists label the newest age group as "The Bridger" generation because they are coming of age in two different centuries. Persons born in 1984 or later are additionally called "The Millennials," the "Internet Generation," and "Generation Y."[38]

I asked each group to describe an ideal worship experience. The Builders prefer hymns, anthems, and traditional gospel music. Baby Boomers like a combination of gospel music and some hymns. Busters seek a deeply personal worship experience; they equate worship with a life coaching or therapy session. And finally, the rap song "Pump Up the Volume"[39] describes what the Bridges desire for worship—very loud contemporary gospel music. A challenger quickly interrupted the process and said, "Pastor, you mean to tell me that not everyone wants to experience worship from my viewpoint?" I replied, "You are correct." He said, "Pastor, we have four different congregations under one roof. It must be challenging trying to move our congregation forward with these kinds of dynamics."

I asked him, "Brother Harry, would you be willing to listen to some loud and different worship music to keep your grandson here?" Then, I asked his grandson, "Would you be willing to listen to hymns and anthems to keep your grandfather here?" Brother Harry said in turn, "Pastor, you are trying to say that we must be flexible." In response, I told him, "Yes. My mother cooked food for the whole house. She didn't cook selected meals for each person. Some days I loved the meal and some days I did not. However, I did know that one day she would get around to my favorite meal." I summarized my job as informing the Oakdale church family that "worship is about GOD and not YOU!"

Brother Harry's acquiescence to our new direction did not take place in response to preaching. It resulted from a combination of spiritual practices. On a number of occasions, he shared his growing appreciation for workshops on change and transition and dynamic translations of biblical passages. He said these Christian Education offerings helped to depersonalize the transition process and shift the blame from the Pastor to Almighty God. In Brother Harry's succinct and

---

38 Gary McIntosh, *One Church, Four Generations: Understanding and Reaching All Ages In Your Church,* (Grand Rapids: Baker Book House Co., 2002) 162.
39 MARRS. *Pump Up the Volume.* Fouth and B'Way, 1990. CD.

sage words, "Pastor, it is hard to fight what God is doing." With the research from our commission on worship and our TMG, we were able to create a worship experience that was (and continues to be) flexible enough to meet our worship needs.

CHAPTER 13

COORDINATE YOUR PREACHING WITH YOUR TRANSITION GOALS

Approaching our church's transitional issues with a clear understanding of the power of preaching, I did not have an effective plan for addressing them. During my first residency in my Doctor of Ministry in Preaching program, I recognized the potential of preaching to allay the congregation's fear and resolve the myriad challenges of transition. My thesis project served the dual purpose of helping improve my preaching and providing essential direction for our pastoral transition. The three years of my doctoral studies also uncovered latent factors that hindered our progress as pastor and people in the transition zone. Moreover, viable transitional solutions emerged, and preaching became a major venue for the exploration of those solutions.

Along with the congregation, I considered preaching to be an indispensable component of pastoral transitional ministry. I minister in the context of an African-American congregation affiliated with a denomination that emphasizes the Holy Scriptures as our primary theological resource in preaching. Rooted in the moderate evangelical tradition, Oakdale Covenant Church desires to apply our Scripture study to daily life. The foundation of our faith, the Bible, shapes relationships between pastor and parishioner. Therefore, pastors in the transition zone must see preaching as one of the major catalysts for navigating transition and positioning the ministry for revival and growth.

Oakdale, along with many congregations, values preaching the Word of God as the most important event in the life of the church. As preaching occurs during Sunday morning worship, the most well-attended of the congregation's weekly events, the sermon uniquely assists congregants with understanding sensitive issues and helping them correlate their challenges with the Scriptures. Pastors must understand that preaching can motivate people to change behavior and inform their expectations as members of the Body of Christ, but preaching can also frustrate a congregation. As the primary vehicle for transmitting God's revelation to the people, sermons disclose a pastor's personality, beliefs, vision, and passion. I would argue that successful transitional preaching determines whether a pastor and parishioners develop a sufficiently strong connection to work together toward a new vision of ministry.

Therefore, pastors must ground their preaching in stalwart biblical and theological notions, as they firmly believe God reveals a lot about transition in the Bible. Pastors can apply the principles of biblical transition stories to our contemporary transitional concerns. For example, the stories about the children of Israel transitioning from slavery in Egypt to the wilderness years and then to the Promised Land offer countless applicable principles. These narratives provide excellent models for pastors and congregations in assessing Almighty God's sovereign and mysterious action during transition.

Since the majority of the congregation attends weekly worship services, preaching afforded an opportunity to name the proverbial "elephants in the room" relating to transitional concerns. Sermons can assure the congregation that God will guide pastor and people through the daunting process of transition and renewal. Preaching further allows pastors to demonstrate their respect for the congregation's history and identity. My preaching gave me an opportunity to convey to the congregation my deep respect for their history and identity. In listening to the biblical origins and foundations of transition, the congregation began to accept change as an intricate part of the spiritual journey. Yet I reassured them of God's changeless nature, which reveals His daily faithfulness in practical ways upon which they could genuinely rely as we traversed the frightening waters of transition. Preaching enables pastors to share that God is very present within transition, orchestrating their moves as they become the congregation He desires.

Exploring New Ways to Prepare a Sermon

In addition to working with the TMG, pastors should take a more systematic approach to sermon preparation and consider redesigning their delivery methods. As a result, pastors should consider strategically planning their preaching in increments of six months. However, pastors must also remain keenly aware of the congregational life cycles and the larger social and political context. Throughout our transition, I regularly asked the Transition Ministry Group, "What major issues are surfacing in our transition and how can the sermon properly address them?" This question and its answers enabled my preaching to have an even greater impact on our transition. This approach allowed me to become more proactive rather than reactive.

As pastors are preparing to preach in the transition zone they should consider structuring each sermon's design by asking these questions: (1) How do I demonstrate God's gracious and mighty acts to His people today and (2) How do I connect Scripture to their life situations in a meaningful and practical way?[40] Primarily, I sought a worthwhile connection between and the infinite God of the universe and my very human parishioners. From the initial premise to the conclusion, pastors must declare an all-powerful God who will faithfully aid His people through any transition.

Additionally, pastors in the transition zone should utilize the celebrative design method of preaching: situation — complication — resolution — celebration as the most helpful approach.[41] This method motivates people through positive reinforcement of the Gospel, which affirms love, joy, hope, and celebration.[42] Sermons with this structure

---

40 Cleophus James LaRue, *Power in the Pulpit: How America's Most Effective Black Preachers Prepare Their Sermons* (Louisville: Westminster John Knox Press, 2002) 19.
41 Frank A. Thomas, *They Like to Never Quit Praisin' God: The Role of Celebration in Preaching* (Cleveland: The Pilgrim Press, 1997) 74-75.
42 Thomas, 45, 74-75.

help congregations celebrate God's presence and direction in their transition.

Narrative preaching can become a third resource in navigating the transition zone. This preaching approach appealed to me because I use many stories when preaching. The late Don Hewitt, longstanding producer of CBS "60 Minutes," stated, "We learned that viewers are not interested in issues, but stories of people whom the issues touch." The people of the Bible were smart enough to talk about issues in the form of stories. Biblical characters embed their wisdom in stories. Old and New Testament narratives offer great metaphors and similes for everyday living while the gospels reflect the absolute need for Jesus Christ in a person's life. Furthermore, biblical stories demonstrate how we can adapt similar moral and ethical principles during times of transition. For example, Israel's transition during the arduous wandering through the wilderness to the Promised Land of Canaan records countless conflicts, but resulted in a most favorable resolution settlement in the land flowing with milk and honey. This preaching method reminds the congregation in transition that even the transitions of biblical characters and groups were not without conflict as they moved towards their goal of survival.

Although narrative preaching was the most effective method for Oakdale's transition, it is not the only sermonic approach. Other preaching methods may include experiencing the richness of the pastoral letters and Gospels through numerous sermons and illustrations. For example, preaching through the book of Acts can help give a congregation insight into successes and challenges of the Early Church. Yet for Oakdale, congregational surveys and TMG feedback yielded the assessment that the most impactful sermons were those that closely followed biblical stories. One parishioner wrote, "Pastor, your preaching resembles a therapy session. When I feel nervous about all these changes and am wondering where God is, you declare a powerful word from the Lord to remind me of God's control of our transition."

Preaching that Communicates Respect, Trust, and Willingness to Listen

To further our transitional goals, I determined that my sermons would always address three critical factors that surfaced in TMG sessions, congregational meetings, and survey results: respect, trust, and listening. The congregation desired that I genuinely address these factors as a condition for its support. The TMG and I reasoned these factors should not be addressed in a congregational letter, Bible Study, or workshop. Preaching is the preferable venue since it reaches a larger audience and the entire congregation needed to hear my thoughts and remarks.

It is important to affirm the maxim that "people do not care about what you know until they know you care." The congregation did not want to hear my vision until they felt my connection. I consequently delayed any preaching or teaching on vision until I sufficiently addressed respect, trust, and listening. Mysteriously, preaching about transition allowed Oakdale and me to go back to the beginning of their movie. The information we gleaned from this experience became an anchor for future change, thereby setting the stage for a stronger reception of my vision for ministry.

Respect

Similar to Oakdale's need for assurance of my respect for its history, legacy, and current leadership, pastors in the transition zone must understand that their congregants are also seeking reassurance that they are respected. For pastors following a long-tenured leader who was deeply admired, this notion of respect is extremely important. The respect factor was important to the people of Oakdale because they had a lengthy and successful experience with my predecessor, and some congregants feared that I would try to ignore or destroy his accomplishments. In addressing this "respect factor," I preached a sermon, "What Kind of Legacy Are You Leaving?" (II Kings 2: 9-11). It illustrates Elijah, the elder prophet, passing the mantle to his younger colleague, Elisha, who accordingly receives a double portion of his spirit as he matures in ministry. The impartation of the senior prophet's spirit enables young Elisha to accomplish greater miracles than his predecessor. I articulated my honor of Oakdale's past successes and leadership, earnestly requesting a double portion of the spirit of our Pastor Emeritus. Humbly, I attempted to demonstrate my respect for and honor of Oakdale's history by asking for "a double portion" of the spirit of our Pastor Emeritus and others so that we could be empowered effectively to face the future of Oakdale with as much strength and courage as they faced in the past. This sermon was important because it allowed the congregation to understand my level of respect for my predecessor and the history of Oakdale. Pastors in the transition zone must constantly convey their respect for the congregation's history. Regularly, I told Oakdale of my respect, but most of all, they needed to know that God providentially blessed the previous ministry of Oakdale, especially their sacrifices to build His kingdom on earth, and that God would bless us.

After the foregoing sermon, I reflected on congregational comments. I obtained a greater appreciation for the importance of respect. One member shared, "Pastor, your sermon helped me to see you have a lot of love and respect for Pastor Jemison. It is so wonderful you both get along so well." Another person commented, "Pastor, your sermon really touched me. I must really admit that I had a problem with your leadership because I felt that you were ignoring the contributions of Pastor Jemison. However, when you said that you wanted 'a double portion of Pastor Jemison's spirit,' I felt that you really and truly care about our Pastor Emeritus." Previously, I had not realized how a few words of affection could significantly, radically, and rapidly change people's opinions. I earnestly prayed, "My God, the preaching moment is a powerful time in the life of the church. Please help me to use it responsibly."[43]

---

43 Darrell Griffin, Journal Entry, (Chicago, IL: January 2004).

Trust

Beyond respect, pastors in the transition zone will find that preaching about trust can be very difficult because it involves transparency. New relationships, whether personal or professional, require a period of establishing communication and building trust. A great deal of distrust existed during my first year at Oakdale. Often, I overheard suspicious comments such as, "Do we really know this young man? Should we trust him with our ministry? Will he hurt us?" Pastors in the beginning of a transition zone should understand that there will be long periods of distrust and uneasiness.

Consequently, pastors must infuse many of their sermons with biblical references relating to trust. One sermon I preached to set the stage for defusing Oakdale's trust factor was titled "God's Unusual Choice," which detailed God's choice of David as King of Israel. This sermon reminded those who did not agree with my appointment as Pastor of Oakdale that although I was not their choice, their fellow congregants had determined that I was God's choice. As prayer, discernment, and evaluation were main components in their pastoral selection process, they then must trust that I was the person whom Almighty God chose to be the pastor for this season of Oakdale's life.

Additionally, while developing sermons on trust, I began to share my personal story. This autobiographical sharing was more effective than pleading, "Please trust me." I recounted experiences about handling difficult people, responding to individuals or groups with whom I differed, making tough decisions and determining directions for ministry. These stories conveyed indirectly to the congregation that their pastor was trustworthy. It gave them a clear picture of a trustworthy leader.

I also talked often about my call to ministry and my passion for evangelism and Christian Education. TMG responses and congregational feedback revealed that many church members found my personal stories and illustrations to be very helpful in shaping their opinions regarding whether they could trust me. One TMG member responded in a session, "I personally am relieved you know how to handle difficult people because there a number of them in our congregation." Another team member said during a "From the Heart of the Pastor" session, "It was nice to hear in your sermon a few weeks ago that you are willing to share some of your power and not be a dictator."

Listening

Pastors in the transition zone should never underestimate the power of listening. Preaching gives pastors an opportunity to show the congregation they are listening to their concerns. Understanding this information, I proactively incorporated into sermons issues that I gleaned from focus group sessions, church board meetings, or congregational meetings. One particular concern surrounded the topic that an increase in worship attendance in a relatively short period of time had inevitably led to an influx of new members. Whereas many members enthusiastically welcomed these new brothers and sisters into our church family, their arrival alarmed a large segment of "old" members. I heard their misgivings in the hallways. "Pastor, do we really know these new people? Should they be allowed to work in our church? We should be doing some background checks on some of these new people." To respond to their heartfelt anxieties, I delivered a sermon, "The People God Uses" (Joshua 2:1-24), centered on the story of Rahab, a prostitute and successful businesswoman.

This sermon emphasizes God's use of persons who had very challenging pasts. Many new members were in recovery programs or had experienced personal traumas. The sermon offered two benefits: first, additional reassurance that I was listening to congregational concerns and, second, the more significant reassurance that God continually listens as well. God reminds us in Scripture that He mysteriously and providentially uses anyone.

Shortly after this sermon, the TMG feedback amazed me. "Pastor, thank you for reminding us that we all have something in our past that we are not proud of, yet God has chosen to use us." Additionally, "Wow,

Pastor, I am relieved to know that your ministry recognizes that church is a hospital for sinners and not a rest home for saints."

Pastors in the transition zone must understand that it is important to listen between the lines and hear what people do not say. The Bible places particular emphasis on the necessity of listening, especially before we speak. Proverbs 19:20 says, "Hear counsel, and receive instruction, that thou mayest be wise in thy latter end." Proverbs 23:19 says, "Hear thou, my son, and be wise, and guide thine heart in the way." Isaiah 55:10-11 says, "For as the rain cometh down, and the snow from heaven, and returneth not thither, but watereth the earth, and maketh it bring forth and bud, that it may give seed to the sower, and bread to the eater: So shall my word be that goeth forth out of my mouth: it shall not return unto me void, but it shall accomplish that which I please, and it shall prosper in the thing whereto I sent it."[44]

Pastors will discover that preaching reveals God's presence in all dimensions of transition. It empowers pastors to reshape the pastoral transition from a frightening experience to a wonderful and joy-filled journey leading to new vistas in ministry. Moreover, weekly sermons supply much-needed reassurance of God's comforting presence during the grief, turbulence, and fear transitions cause. Another member of the TMG remarked, "Addressing the fear factors in your sermons really helped to curb many fears and questions." Yet another survey respondent offered, "Pastor, your sermons have really given me unique insight into your life and love for our church. Keep on guiding us with God's Word." Summarily, this comment from an anonymous congregant captured my preaching objective: "Pastor, your preaching has not answered all of Oakdale's fears, but you have demonstrated how to take the Word of God and apply it to our lives and situations so we can find our own answers from God."

Pastors who coordinate their preaching with their transitional goals will have a tremendous advantage in the transition zone. It will allow them to have preaching tools and resources to go back to the beginning

---

44 King James Version, Proverbs 19:20, Proverbs 23:19 and Isaiah 55:10-11.

of their congregation's movie and use the information as an anchor for changing the future and setting the stage for a stronger reception to ministry vision.

CHAPTER 14

BE WARY OF TRANSITION FATIGUE SYNDROME

Oakdale was winding down its turbulent tenure in the transition zone and repositioning itself to launch a new beginning when suddenly, without warning, a threat to the very future of the ministry appeared. The interesting aspect of this threat was that it was difficult to identify because it was buried beneath our successes. From the outside looking in, Oakdale appeared to have successfully navigated the worst of its transition zone. The most difficult challenges seemed to be behind us and we were ready to re-launch a new vision for an even stronger Oakdale.

The membership grew significantly, increasing from 800 to over 2,000. We weathered the frightening storms of changing our worship style from a traditional liturgy to a more contemporary experience. The tremendous growth attracted young families, which strengthened our children's and youth ministries. We were meeting the needs of our growing congregation through the expansion of programming from 40 to well over 70 ministries. The resignation of several lay leaders, whom I perceived were hindering progress, created opportunities for new leaders with commitment, competence, energy, and openness to emerge. Slowly, we built a team committed to the implementation of new ideas. In many ways, we were thriving beyond our expectations; we could not imagine more favorable circumstances. Leaders in the surrounding community regularly commented on Oakdale's numerical and programmatic growth. As we transitioned, Oakdale became a healthier congregation with a new commitment to missions, outreach, and empowering our local community.

However, a serious threat to future success had been overlooked inadvertently as we planned our transition strategies. Whereas the TMG and other leaders had considered a number of other possible challenges, we were not quite ready for people becoming just plain tired of changes and growth. In fact, the pastor, lay leadership and congregation were feeling physically, mentally, and spiritually fatigued. We had not prepared to be inflicted with what I call Transition Fatigue Syndrome.

Transition Fatigue Syndrome surfaces when a congregation changes so rapidly that people are unable to fully adjust before making another change. As the congregation was embracing these shifts on policies and procedures, we were asking them to make even more adaptations physically, mentally, and spiritually.

We quickly discovered that Transition Fatigue Syndrome was one of the most detrimental forces to a congregation's ability to navigate change and launch its new beginning. This forced us to decrease the pace of transition efforts as the congregation was in a most fragile state. Utilizing Bridges' characterization of transition phases of ending, wilderness, and new beginning, Oakdale was in the fragile wilderness stage. Oakdale was no longer in the ministry era of the Pastor Emeritus, yet we had not embraced fully the ministerial vision that I offered. We languished within an interim period of spiritual wilderness, wandering and journeying through the transition zone without clarity as a church. The hurried pace of moving and changing caused Oakdale's identity to shift, resulting in an identity crisis.

As Oakdale's membership constantly increased and necessary changes were implemented, many long-term parishioners feared the loss of the church's identity. In some instances, these parishioners forthrightly resisted any changes because they were unsure about the type of congregation we would have after the transition. The "small family church" orientation was evolving into large church mindset. Undoubtedly, this shift would mean the loss of personal connections with the pastor and lay leaders. As this new church identity was unsettling for many people, an antigrowth mentality surfaced. Any additional changes were perceived as a mechanism to promote growth, and promoting growth was viewed as pushing Oakdale from its family-oriented identity to an uncomfortable new one.

It was difficult to accept this indiscriminate resistance, as change always occurs in any congregation's landscape. In fact, to survive and thrive continually, a congregation must change. Ironically, the most needed changes create the greatest risks, which in turn foster tremendous anxiety within a congregation. In this era of constant change, identifying and preventing Transition Fatigue Syndrome is critical. If it is not addressed, fear motivates people to burn out after the smallest changes. The congregation lacks the energy to defend the status quo or navigate necessary changes. As a consequence, preventing and managing fatigue is a critical component of pastoral leadership during transition.

One method of addressing valid concerns about nonstop change is to postpone any non-essential changes. Spend more time researching the landscape of the congregation to anticipate its future needs.[45] In doing so, pastors will encourage the congregation to grasp that transition is a journey and not a destination.

The TMG deserves credit for labeling Oakdale's Transition Fatigue Syndrome. After naming this powerful emotional force that permeated the congregation, we concluded that the majority of Oakdale members did not want to halt or sabotage progress. They simply needed periods for rest, reflection, and renewal. Once we discovered that Oakdale was experiencing Transition Fatigue Syndrome, we devised a strategy for effectively reducing the deadly consequences of fatigue. Today, we continue to employ this tactic to guide our transitions and prevent any future outbreaks of Transition Fatigue Syndrome.

Strategies for Reducing Transition Fatigue Syndrome

One of the biggest strategies we discovered was that regular communication significantly reduced Transition Fatigue Syndrome. Potentially, communication is a double-edged sword that can either

---

45 Bridges, 103.

raise readiness for change and reduce resistance, or raise resistance and reduce readiness. Pastors and leaders often make two fundamental mistakes when communicating in the transition zone. First, they give very little information too late, believing they have nothing to say or, second, they share incomplete information too soon before all the plans are complete. Both approaches raise anxiety levels and foster greater resistance, yet the failure to communicate openly, honestly, and in a timely manner is equally disastrous.

In times of uncertainty, people seek clarity and reliable information.[46] Therefore, if you do not communicate, you increase the likelihood of someone disseminating erroneous information. The result is the potential for resistance to change to create fertile ground for the church "grapevine" to overflow with rumors. Any leader who fails to communicate loses control of the message. Why does this matter? Whereas congregants will accept uncritically even the most outrageous rumors from an unofficial source, the pastor and leadership must share ideas or vision repeatedly and in several different ways before individuals will receive it.

Again, I want to caution pastors and leaders as it relates to giving too much information too soon. While it is indeed necessary to communicate important developments, it is equally imperative to remember that "important" does not automatically mean "helpful." Striking this balance is critical so that you communicate at the congregation's level of readiness. Consider the emotional response of the majority of individuals affected by change, and think about their ability to process the information in a supportive way.

To avoid these two common mistakes, the TMG and I created a communication framework. Implemented at the beginning of any new initiative, this framework aligns knowledge and individuals to successfully communicate within the continuum of change. It designs a fluid mechanism for exchanging information on individual and collective scales as people progress through change.

---

46 Bridges,103.

Russ Olmon, President of Ministry Advantage,[47] a ministry coaching company, and my personal ministry coach, suggested Oakdale develop a systematic approach to communicating about change rather than offering updates about a string of unrelated ministry changes. A holistic approach allows the congregation to recognize connections and how changes will affect the entire congregation. Olmon additionally suggested a visual transition map using charts, graphs, timelines, and symbols to track current and future changes as well as to evaluate their impact on the congregation.

To implement Olmon's suggestions, we regularly monitored the congregation's progress through the transition process with focus groups, town hall meetings, surveys, and other ministry evaluative instruments, ensuring organizational alignment within the TMG and lay leadership while also helping to reduce transition fatigue. We consistently engaged those persons most affected by the transition, as these individuals are often the greatest asset or liability to the success of the ministry. Accordingly, it is simply wise to include them throughout the planning and facilitation of transitional moves.

47 "Ministry Advantage – About Us," 2012 http://www.ministryadvantage.org/index.cfm/PageID/2559/index.html.

CHAPTER 15

PREACHING THROUGH
TRANSITION FATIGUE SYNDROME

Throughout this book I have emphasized the importance of relevant preaching during a period of transition. This includes preaching that addresses Transition Fatigue Syndrome. This chapter provides two examples of sermons for preaching through Transition Fatigue Syndrome.

Sermon Example One: "Stand Still"

This sermon identified our challenges. In defining our experience of Transition Fatigue Syndrome, we had to assure the congregation of God's definite presence within our pastoral transition. I preached a sermon series to describe the wilderness stage of our journey. Detailing the children of Israel's transition journey from slavery in Egypt through the Red Sea crossing and then to the wilderness stage served as a model to help us see God's handiwork in our confusion. The exegetical and hermeneutical insights of Exodus 14:1-14 were spiritual manna, quail, and water as we experienced this wilderness phase. In fact, the book of Exodus records Israel's transition from slavery to freedom. The first through fourteenth chapters reveal God's faithful provision and His divine purpose in every aspect of the transition journey.

As people in transition, the Israelites faced a critical decision in the wilderness. Would they psychologically, mentally, and spiritually leave their slave experience in Egypt and embrace their new freedom as they journeyed toward the Promised Land? After 450 years of exposure to Egyptian gods, culture and amenities, could the children of Israel envision a new life? Surrounded by the bare necessities and unfamiliarity of the wilderness with its limited supply of bread, meat, and water, they lived at a juncture directly between their past slavery and future promises made by Almighty God to their forebears. Would they pull back and retreat to the comforts of Egypt or transition into the Promised Land?

Numerous daily challenges regarding food, shelter and survival combined to aggravate their transition journey toward freedom. These constant changes in directions and instructions as they followed the pillar of cloud by day and a pillar of fire by night caused many Israelites to experience transition fatigue. They were unaccustomed to following the divine and holy instructions of one God. After all, Egypt had a deity for practically every daily activity. Therefore, God directed Moses to instruct the children of Israel to "stand still and see the salvation of the Lord."

I paralleled this biblical account to Oakdale's experience. As we transitioned into God's will for us at the beginning of the 21st century, we were in the wilderness. Some congregants were comfortable as they sought to extend the years of my predecessor. Others accepted the hard reality that we had to embrace the sociological, political, and technological challenges of the new millennium. Still others felt caught in the middle of these disparate visions of ministry. Suffice it to say that many members of Oakdale found this wilderness period of questioning, change, and adaptation to be rather difficult and unsettling. Multiple changes eroded our comfort zone. As Murphy's Law predictably influenced our transition and our best laid plans did not come to fruition, matters only worsened. Unsurprisingly, some congregants cried aloud, "Let's go back! Let's go back to what we used to do! We know that works! Pastor, were there no graves in Egypt? Pastor, why did you take us from what we were comfortable with and lead us to the middle of nowhere? You have us going the long way. It doesn't make sense to 'stand still and see the Salvation of the Lord.' You are backtracking. You are killing the church. Let's go back while we can."

Moses issues a command under girded by a divine promise to help the Israelites with their fears of transition. Were Oakdale to heed these enduring biblical instructions, I posited we would progress successfully toward new vistas in ministry and building the Kingdom of God on earth. First, like Moses, we would have to persevere in faith. He relied on God's everlasting faithfulness. Moses recalled the burning bush experience and realized God's lasting provision since that day. Likewise, Oakdale would need to trust God's orchestration of every detail in our transition. Second, we had to stop panicking and being afraid. Fear kills dreams and adventure. It leads to blame, rather than analysis, when mistakes occur. The children of Israel accused "Pastor Moses" of causing their distress. Moreover, fear erased any memories of God's past faithfulness. I cautioned Oakdale about fear's tendency to eclipse God's presence. Third, I shared our need to rest in His comfort and power as we "stand still and see the Salvation of the Lord." He will reveal His purpose. Ironically, standing still and waiting for His guidance can be our greatest action.

Monumental revelations emerge only when we discard the busyness of life by standing still and listening attentively to God. His presence empowers us with courage and strength for the balance of our journey. "He giveth power to the faint and to them who have no might, He increaseth strength." (Isaiah 40:29)[48] Fourth, I reminded Oakdale that God is ever-present, which means in practical terms that He is present with us each day. He will intervene favorably on our behalf when we are least expectant, usually when we have exhausted ourselves. Through Moses, God assured the Israelites that "the Egyptians whom you have seen today you will never see again, forever." The Lord fought their battle and He will fight similarly for us if we are willing to stand still. Additionally, God's deliverance is not always physical. Often, He liberates us mentally and spiritually before we can enjoy physical freedom.

---

48 King James Version, Isaiah 40:29.

Celebration and Experience in Preaching, by Henry H. Mitchell, supplied my sermon techniques. Mitchell's description of narrative sermons is particularly helpful. "The narrative in the sermon can be defined like any other good story, except that it is told with the purpose of winning souls to Christ, helping them to grow, and motivating them to serve. The standard components of a story are required: setting, cast, plot, conflict and resolution."[49]

This method engages listeners as they discover meaning in the Scriptures through a narrative sequence. Utilizing this homiletical strategy, I personify the main character, which thinks, feels, and speaks as humanly as the people sitting in the pews. In my first sermon relating to transition, I depicted the vivid setting of Egypt, the wilderness, and the Red Sea. Two major conflicts arise in the narrative: Pharaoh's resistance to liberating the children of Israel and their subsequent struggle with monotheism after 450 years of polytheism in Egypt. Assuming Moses' disposition, I articulated the paradoxical resolution to "stand still and see the Salvation of the Lord."

Mitchell's celebrative design method of preaching is equally beneficial. This technique enthusiastically celebrates God's triumphant actions in the narrative and the world. The congregation rejoiced with me as they understood that God's gracious deliverance for Israel meant that He would perform similarly for Oakdale. "Standing still" is not a weak response to adversity. Instead, it is an appeal for divine empowerment. Beyond this episode at the Red Sea, many biblical characters utilize a method to receive God's assistance in the midst of their most personal and private crucible of pain and suffering.

Thomas H. Troeger's *Preaching While the Church is Under Reconstruction* is another helpful preaching resource. He stresses the importance of connecting a church's context to preaching. As each congregation is as different as each person, it is important that preachers understand a church's unique traditions and setting.

---

49 Henry H. Mitchell, *Celebration and Experience in Preaching* (Nashville: Abingdon Press, 1990) 40-41.

In response, I carefully studied Oakdale's culture, politics, and relational landscape. My research gave me very valuable insight into how Oakdale handles transitions. Bridges' work helped to identify where Oakdale was on the pastoral transition trajectory. Appreciating distinctions between the external nature of change and the emotional processes that arise within transition enabled me to choose my next steps more wisely.

Oakdale actually was letting go of her old identity and ministry methods as she progressed toward a neutral zone. Bridges states, "Just when you decided that the hardest part of managing transition is getting people to let go of the old ways, you enter a state of affairs in which neither the old ways nor the new ways work satisfactorily. People are caught between the demands of conflicting systems and end up immobilized."[50] The neutral zone potentially strengthens or destroys a ministry as decision making appears unclear, purpose seems lacking, and activities look aimless. Confusion expands and anxieties build as congregants desperately want a definite and concrete new beginning instead of a promise. Interestingly, these powerful emotions can threaten the next phase of ministry.

To more accurately gauge the congregation's response to my sermons regarding pastoral transition, the TMG designed a questionnaire consisting of six inquiries, which it distributed to 75 members:.

1. What was the sermon's main theme?
2. What did you like about the sermon?
3. What didn't you like about the sermon?
4. Were there things you think Pastor needed to add to this sermon?
5. Have you witnessed any changes in Pastor's preaching? If so, what?
6. Are there any areas in Pastor's preaching that need improving? If yes, what?

The members of the TMG aggressively encouraged the congregation to complete and return the questionnaire. As a result of their hard work,

---

50 Bridges, 35.

nearly half of the surveys were returned. The findings revealed that a majority of members appreciated how the sermon "Stand Still" was crafted to allow the text to speak to our current transition issues.

Sermon Sample Two: "The Power of Rest"

This sermon addressed our personal and collective feelings resulting from constant change. In order to assuage Oakdale's transition fatigue, the second sermon focused on the value of Sabbath, which I will characterize as rest henceforth. God does not desire endless labor, however positive and beneficial, without regular periods of rest. Thus, we needed to build breaks into our transitional process. In establishing the Sabbath after creation in Genesis 2:1-3, God models a balance between work (whether secular or spiritual) and rest. I entitled this sermon "The Power of Rest." In addition, I conducted a Bible study series on the significance of rest in the midst of a pastoral transition. We needed to ease the mounting strain of rapid change and its physical, emotional, and spiritual toll on the congregation.

Intentionally, I used the word "rest" rather than "Sabbath." For most parishioners, Sabbath conjures images of Sunday as a holy day reserved exclusively for morning worship. Consequently, a sizeable majority of the congregation misses the need for physical, mental, and relational renewal and relaxation. Therefore, I delved deeply into exegetical and hermeneutical insights in order to unpack the word "Sabbath" and its practical meaning of pausing and resting.

Again, in Genesis 2:1-3, God demonstrates the necessity of rest. After spending six days creating the earth, animals and plant life, solar systems, stars, and the infinite expanse of the universe, God rests from all work on the seventh day. God blesses the seventh day and makes it holy. This passage institutes this important and powerful spiritual discipline that disciples need to practice as much today as they ever have. Quite simply, if the all-powerful, ever-present, all-kind, and all-knowing Lord of the universe had to rest, then it is elemental that we, His handiwork, would need to rest as well.

122

The Incarnation maintains this commandment. Often, the Lord Jesus Christ withdrew from the crowds in order to spend time alone with the Father.[51] Strikingly, Jesus withdraws when He is most in demand. He is not being self-indulgent; Jesus understands that human need is endless. In order to accomplish His Messianic and salvific purpose, He must remain spiritually strong, which requires a daily routine of prayer, meditation, rest and recuperation.

For this sermon I concentrated on five key points: First, rest allows us to listen to God. Easily, the cacophony of life with the competing demands of marriage, parenting, and pastoral ministry with their rising and sustained crescendos drowns out the still, small voice of God. Interestingly, as pastors, we are often so busy doing things for Christ that we forget to simply be with Christ. Second, rest reminds us of our human limitations and better enables us to actualize our divine potential. As we meditate when resting, we acquire more humility because we learn not to take ourselves so seriously. Third, with the balanced perspective we gain from physical rest, we realize that some situations are not as dramatic, significant, and traumatic as we think when we are mentally and physically exhausted. Fourth, a period of withdrawal from normal responsibilities without cell phones, e-mail, and other technological distractions demonstrates that we are not as indispensable as we imagine. Fifth and finally, rest encourages us to step off life's treadmill and exchange unproductive habits with "holy hope" where we are able to reconnect with the roots of our soul.

Again, the TMG played a significant role in the development of this sermon. The members of the TMG fully agreed that constant changes over a four-year period had caused the congregation to experience transition fatigue. Half of the TMG expressed personal feelings of fatigue. I acknowledged the strain of non-stop change throughout this sermon, which gave the congregation spiritual permission to rest. They better understood Sabbath as a necessary part of our transition journey.

---

51 Luke 5:15-16 and Mark 1:35-36.

To more accurately gauge the congregation's response to my sermons relating to pastoral transition, the TMG once again utilized a survey. The findings were encouraging. This sermon confirmed our beliefs about the side effects of constant change. Many people did not know how to express their feelings without guilt or shame. They were relieved to know that God never desired for us to transition continually without rest and rejuvenation. One respondent wrote that the sermon was "a breath of fresh air for Oakdale and deeply needed. Thanks." Other congregants considered this sermon to be my most practical one, as it was very easy to follow and apply. Finally, a few persons noted that the sermon incorporated more Scriptural references than usual.

I agree that "The Power of Rest" was my most practical sermon. I wanted the congregation to appreciate the importance of rest without traipsing through any deep theological thoughts. Particularly, I observed that the congregation's reaction was more reflective, yet I felt an emotional connection with them while delivering this sermon.

This sermon signaled a new direction for our ministry. In response, four members of the church board suggested that each ministry find resources to balance their work and rest. I shared this suggestion with the congregation at a quarterly congregational business meeting. Overwhelmingly, we agreed that each ministry should implement this practice.

CHAPTER 16

MANAGING CONFLICT IN THE TRANSITION ZONE

I could not conclude this book without addressing the issue of conflict. Few issues trouble our faith as persistently as tension between pastors and lay leaders relating to collaboratively navigating ministerial transitions. As parishioners become increasingly stressed over the new direction of the ministry, these opposing views cause conflict between them to surface. Not surprisingly, a chasm between pastor and congregation also widens. Circumstances naturally hurl pastors and lay leaders into transition zones with little preparation or resources for navigating this impasse. Without willingness to learn from and with each other, pastors and leaders can possibly destroy healthy congregations. The African proverb I cited earlier bears repeating: "When two elephants fight, only the grass suffers." When pastors and leaders fight aimlessly, the church suffers. In consequence, the pastor loses focus, the congregation stops listening to the pastor or the leadership, and very few people are accomplishing Christ's evangelistic work.

The destructive force of water best symbolizes conflict's effect on a congregation. It spills over, flows downhill, and eventually erodes whatever it touches. Defined as "open and hostile opposition resulting from differing viewpoints," conflict is not synonymous with disagreement. Hostility does not normally emerge from disagreements. Conflict usually produces hostility, as people on opposite sides of an issue unrelentingly insist on having their way.

According to the Bible, the nature of conflict arises from selfish desires and conflicting agendas (James 4:1). Individuals and groups desiring to blindly push their ideas, goals, and passions are what fuels conflict. As these individuals or groups force their positions or ideas, many do so by discrediting others, leaving the environment very toxic. In some insistences the pastor and a few leaders are guilty of stirring the conflict pot by pursing their own personal agendas rather than following God's will. Such conflict is contrary to God's Word, which instructs "If it is possible, as far as it depends on you live at peace with everyone." (Romans 12:18)[52] In fact, the New Testament in particular gives a number of examples and commands about how to treat others.

A majority of the conflict we experienced at Oakdale was the product of changing times and also the fact that the pastor and the current leadership were caught in dysfunctional and outdated church systems and programs that no longer addressed the changing needs of our congregation or the community. The congregation's growth and its strain on our outdated structures and systems put pressure on the pastor and leadership, creating conflict. Also, our system of decision making involved more than 20 leaders from our church board. Instead of this large group making over-arching policy decisions that would impact the day-to-day operations of the ministry, they were actually directly involved in much of the day-to-day operational decisions. This made it extremely difficult and very time-consuming to build consensus around new ideas, directions, or initiatives. All were blindly focusing on their own viewpoint and spending large amounts of energy discrediting anyone or anything that stood in their way. What added fuel to the fire of our conflict was when both opposing parties were lacing their comments with statements like "God told me" or "God put it upon my heart." When the God-dimension has been added to any argument, it becomes very difficult to build consensus. The constant conflict that would arise because of the many different ideas, agendas, and viewpoints created a near impossible situation to navigate as a pastor. Unlike many business and civic leaders who often have the authority to resolve or remove conflict-causing people, pastors and church leaders are managing conflict and seeking reconciliation with individuals who are volunteers. Thus, pastors

---

52 New International Version, Romans 12:18.

and church leaders are forced to mediate and create environments where disputing individuals can reconcile without destroying the ministry.

As mentioned earlier, I had the distinct privilege of serving as the Assistant Pastor of Abyssinian Baptist Church in Harlem under the pastorate of Dr. Calvin O. Butts, III. He emphasized my need to discern the congregation's feelings particularly as they relate to conflict. He often advised, "Dee, if you ask God for any gift, make sure that it is the gift of discernment." In the difficult periods that arise in pastoral ministry, discernment serves as a pastor's best asset.

However, our constant conflict forced me into seeking skills for teaching and training on conflict management and resolution. Although some people have natural skills for resolving conflict, the majority of us must be intentional about acquiring such necessary skills. After lengthy discussions with our church board and the TMG, we agreed that seeking outside help was a step in the right direction to address and manage our conflict. We needed skills and resources to manage the unhealthy people who were assuming leadership. We also needed someone who could come in and take an objective look at things and help give us a guideline for resolving conflict and creating a healthy environment.

As I was searching for the resources to assist with conflict management, I found very few Christian conferences, workshops, or books that addressed this pressing issue, which has destroyed so many congregations. On the other hand, I found that business and civic leaders have a number of resources at their disposal to manage and resolve conflict. Oakdale is fortunate to be a part of a denomination that offers some resources for resolving and managing conflict. For example, our conference office was helpful in serving as mediators and consultants, and several of our denominational conferences for pastors offered classes around the issue of conflict management and resolution. One of the most helpful resources was a local university that offered a number of classes and workshops on conflict management and resolution. I have discovered that learning how to manage conflict is not an option for pastors and church leaders, but rather a requirement for their success in ministry.

From my classes and workshops on conflict management, I acquired some valuable resources that proved vital for navigating our transition zone and managing our conflict. One resource we used was *Caring Enough to Confront: How to Understand and Express Your Deepest Feelings Toward Others*, by David Augsburger. Augsburger gave us fresh insight into conflict as he writes, "We must see conflict as natural, normal, neutral and sometimes even delightful. Recognize that conflict can turn into painful or disastrous ends, but it doesn't need to. Conflict is neither good nor bad, right nor wrong; conflict simply is."[53]

We had to understand that conflict was a normal part of any community. In fact, from Genesis to Revelation, Scripture is full of incidents of conflict; even our Lord and Savior, Jesus Christ, found Himself leading in the midst of conflict. There is no leadership model that is free of conflict or personality clashes. Therefore, conflict is inescapable. Every leader will encounter resistance to his or her leadership. However, while conflict may be unavoidable, it does not have to be destructive. We discovered that the tension from our conflict could be healthy and beneficial towards our transition and growth. Some of our conflict forced us to change outdated church systems, clarify ministry goals and objectives, improve problem solving, or better manage outcomes. Many of the improvements that occurred at Oakdale grew out of conflict. For example, an outside consultant helped us to develop and implement a new church board structure that helped to streamline decisions and foster a team environment.

Another important lesson I learned regarding conflict pertains to my role and responsibility as pastor. Pastors and church leaders have to learn how to confront a conflicting personality without arguing. Arguments are magnetic for dysfunctional and hostile people because they think that bullying their way toward winning an argument will produce victory or significance for them. Therefore, as pastors we have to learn how to control our behavior, because people who are addicted to conflict and

---

53 David Augsburger, *Caring Enough To Confront: How To Understand And Express Your Deepest Feelings Toward Others* (3rd Ed. Ventura: Regal Publishing, 2009) 11.

chaos can inflict such hurt and injury to produce rage in a person's heart. We have to learn to control ourselves because a loss of control of one's feelings is exactly what hostile people seek. It makes them feel that they are using the right control tactic to take over the situation.

Our research also uncovered that volunteer organizations, and particularly churches, are a haven for people with difficult and challenging personalities. In fact, I would often hear many people refer to the church as a hospital, a place for sick people. Therefore, if the church is referred to as a hospital, then it is full of sick people in need of serious healing and direction. In many cases when people become Christians they do not automatically shed their previous attitudes and demeanor. They simply transfer it to the church. Norman Shawchuck confirms this in an article titled "Staying Cool When the Heat's on: Causes and Cures for Conflict." He states, "Another source of church conflict is the fact the church is a haven for disenfranchised, broken people who may not function well in society. People who do not function well in society often migrate to volunteer organizations because they believe the volunteer organization will care for them. It is one thing to work alongside people who are emotionally healthy, but it is another thing [to work] with people who are emotionally unhealthy. How do we structure our programs and our goals when we are working with people who can sap hours of our time and energy? In a straight-line organization, a non-volunteer organization, they fire them; the church cannot do that. It is important, then, that the pastor be trained to understand volunteer organizations."[54] Our awareness of this fact led us to form partnerships with therapists and counselors to whom we could refer those who have serious psychological and emotional problems.

With this proper understanding of conflict, we were able to anticipate and even manage potential clashes in personalities and ideas and to channel them into creative forces for navigating our transition. We learned how to integrate each other's needs and wants, creating a

---

54 Norman Shawchuck, "Staying Cool When the Heat's On: Causes and Cures for Conflict," *Enrichment Journal* 9 *no. 2* Spring 2005: 32.

wonderful catalyst for deepening our relationship with one another and making us an even stronger team.

Following are some important conflict management tips that we learned while navigating our transition zone:

1. Realize that conflict is natural and happens all the time.
2. Remember that not all conflict is bad. In fact, if handled well, conflict often leads to innovation. It is important to remember that conflict is not inherently destructive. In fact, some conflict is desirable.
3. Develop ground rules and use agendas. The task of managing conflict becomes easier if we have ground rules for airing disagreements. The group must agree on guidelines for communication, negotiation, and decision making. They should agree on the objective of the negotiation process. For example, a ground rule might dictate that different opinions will be heard and respected or that abusive language will not be tolerated. Another example would be that only issues, not personalities, are subjects for debate.
4. Separate people from the problem. We discovered that people have their own unique needs, emotions, and perceptions. Some conflicts are based on differences in thinking and perception. These types of conflict may exist mainly in people's minds.
5. Focus on the real problem, not the symptoms. Find the root cause of the conflict, determining if the dispute is work-related, personal, or both.
6. Don't let conflict linger.
7. Communicate. Conflict is more likely to occur when communication is not clear and when there is confusion about what is valued and rewarded. It seems that nearly all conflict involves some aspect of poor communication. Both verbal and written communication hasboth values and liability.
8. Recognize which conflicts are yours to manage. Fortunately, some conflicts are not the business of the pastor.

My two sons compete on a swimming team and one day I was in the locker room with them just before a competition. There, the coach typically takes a few minutes to talk to his team, among other things, reminding them of their preparation. On this occasion, as the boys sat on the benches anticipating the swim meet, their coach offered this charge: "Tiger Sharks, this is the locker room. It is a place of preparation. It is a place of encouragement. It is a place where mistakes are confronted and corrected. But we can't win a swimming meet in this room. Swimming meets are not won in the locker room. The joy of the game is not felt in the locker room. It's out there in the pool. We have practiced enough. Now let's go out there and win!"

I applied Coach Mike's words to Oakdale's transition. If a coach has done his job well, his team leaves the locker room ready to sacrifice whatever is necessary to win. Although the locker room is a comfortable and safe place to receive instructions and guidance, swimming meets and other athletic contests are never won there. Likewise, transition does not occur in plush sanctuaries. As pastors serve as coaches to their congregations, they will leave planning meetings and worship services to commit to attaining success in the transition zone of daily living. Problematically, many pastors and congregants develop a "locker room mentality" that hinders their participation and progress in the game of evangelism, ministry, and growth. The easier and softer way is to remain in the locker room rather than to practice what we are learning as disciples of the Lord Jesus Christ.

Despite having read the latest book on transition, collected important information from surveys and focus groups, and attended creative conferences on transition and change, any number of congregations remain trapped in a locker room mentality. To avoid "the paralysis of analysis," pastors, lay leaders, and congregations need firm and inviolate deadlines. Courageously, they take the next right steps, embracing risks with versatility to achieve progress.

I pray that reading of the pains and joys of Oakdale's transition will ease your transitional struggles. While I would like to impart a magic formula that works in all transitions, I trust you concur with the book's fundamental premise that navigating the transition zone is too complex for simple solutions. The unique characteristics and context of each transition require careful evaluation, which yields distinct recommendations. Hard work, tough decisions, and very careful attention to God's voice are rudimentary. Unquestionably, with God's guidance, you will successfully navigate the transition zone.

You may recall that in October of 1947 Charles Yeager became the first pilot to break the sound barrier. Many pilots had attempted this feat, but upon reaching the speed of sound with the violent shaking and rattling of the plane, they always pulled back on the plane's throttle. These pilots feared the plane would break apart. In contrast and in the same situation, Captain Yeager pushed forward. Arguably, it was his determination that broke the sound barrier. Afterwards, he discovered the remainder of the flight was smooth.

As you preach and serve in the transition zone, inevitably you will feel the violent shaking and rattling of pastoral and congregational ministry. Your fears will tempt you to pull back. Wholeheartedly, I encourage you to listen attentively to the voice of the Holy Spirit, who will empower you to press forward until you reach smooth skies. I experienced the same thing, and the shaking and rattling certainly tested my resolve. I am most grateful to Almighty God that Oakdale Evangelical Covenant Church is stronger in mission, purpose, and character because we humbly and steadfastly transcended the barriers of our pastoral transition. And I hope this book assists you in cultivating leadership skills, personal courage, and spiritual disciplines to guide you through congregational transitions as you create a visible trail for posterity.

Afterword

The best movies in life are those that capture and hold our imagination, even days after we see them. We don't get the movie, the movie gets us.

The stories told and the principles taught by Dr Griffin continue to resonate with me long after the final page. His words ring true to life and ministry, especially in the context of leading revitalization in an established church. Such a task requires courage, coaching and commitment over the long haul.

The metaphor of walking into the middle of a movie is an accurate description of the realities and complexities of the revitalization challenge. And the metaphors we use greatly influence how we think, feel and behave in a certain situation.

Pastors are wise to follow Dr Griffin's example, especially when it comes to honoring the best of the past, standing on the shoulders of those who have gone before and mastering the delicate art of leading transition. Effective pastors are narrative archeologists; they dig up the radical life giving stories that are locked up in the archives of the church and then re-tell those stories in a way that connects with how the Holy Spirit is moving in the present.

When done well, there is a prevailing culture of trust that develops and the church continues to move forward into the future that God has for them. Yet most leaders are so focused on outcomes that they neglect to start with the real and perceived losses that followers are experiencing. Healthy missional pastors are attuned and sensitive to the grief and loss that naturally accompanies the transition process. And they know how to articulate this inner language of the heart.

They are also aware of their own character development and role as the plot thickens. The journey of revitalization is both adventurous and treacherous. Those pastors who pay attention to and care for their own souls along the journey, provide the kind of authentic Spirit-filled leadership that Christ followers are yearning for. No amount of work *for* the King can replace being *with* the King.

As the pastor believes in the people and the people believe in the pastor…this is when esprit de corp is at its finest and fruitful ministry gets traction. This is when dreams become bigger than memories.

This is when hope wins.

I see this story line lived out every time I visit the Oakdale family… a great church with great people serving a great God!

This book is an awesome resource for pastors and lay leaders who dare to dream again.

John Wenrich
Director of Congregational Vitality
Evangelical Covenant Church

Darrell Griffin
Oakdale Covenant Church
Chicago, IL
Ministry Advantage was able to help us create systems that simplified our ministry and helped us become even more creative and more spirit-centered, and took us even further in our impact on our church and our community.

Russ Olmon
Ministry Advantage
Ministry Advantage has been serving the local church for over a decade. Urban Ministry Advantage was created to address the unique issues in the urban church. I am very excited to have Darrell and Anthony leading the charge for Urban Ministry Advantage.

Anthony Trufant
Emmanuel Baptist Church
Brooklyn, NY
I wish I'd had this resource earlier in my ministry! If you take advantage of the coaching process that Ministry Advantage offers, not only will your ministry be changed, but YOU will be changed.

Ministry Advantage is now offering all church leaders access to the Online Coaching Center. Pastors can not only develop their own personal leadership skills, they can also use the Online Coaching Center to have **unlimited staff and volunteer leaders** in development at the same time. Each leader can have his/her own personal account as part of a **single monthly** paid subscription that belongs to the church. **Personal coaches are available as an additional service.**

PRACTICES
OF **EFFECTIVE** CHURCHES

Strategic Planning
Leading Change
Organization/Delegation
Developing Leaders
Outreach/Assimilation
Raising Resources
Building Teams

URBAN
MINISTRY
ADVANTAGE

ONLINE
CHURCH LEADER DEVELOPMENT
CENTER

800-314-9883
ministryadvantage.org/urban